Liturgy
the Life of the Church

Lambert Beauduin OSB

Liturgy
the Life of the Church

Translated by

Virgil Michel OSB

Third Edition
Saint Michael's Abbey Press
MMII

SAINT MICHAEL'S ABBEY PRESS
Saint Michael's Abbey
Farnborough
Hants. GU14 7NQ

Telephone +44 (0) 1252 546 105
Facsimile +44 (0) 1252 372 822

www.farnboroughabbey.org
prior@farnboroughabbey.org

French Original: *La Piété de L'Église: Principes et Faits,* Abbaye du Mont-César & Abbaye de Maredsous, Louvain 1914.

First and second English editions:
The Liturgical Press, Collegeville, 1926 & 1929.

Third edition:
© Saint Michael's Abbey 2002

ISBN 0 907077 40 4

Cover design – Peter Harden

This book is sold subject to the condition that it shall not, by way of trade or otherwise, be lent, re-sold, hired out or otherwise circulated without the publisher's prior consent in any form of binding or cover other than that in which it is published and without a similar condition including this condition being imposed on the subsequent purchaser.

A catalogue record for this book is available from the British Library.

Printed and bound in Great Britain by Biddles Ltd,
Guildford and King's Lynn.

Table of Contents

Preface   7

Introduction   9

PART ONE
THE RESTORATION OF THE SACRED LITURGY

Chapter I: The Fundamental Principle   13

Chapter II: The Present Condition: the Nature of the Evil   19

Chapter III: The Consequences of the Present Condition   23

Chapter IV: The Advantages of Liturgical Piety   32

Chapter V: The Liturgical Movement   49

PART TWO
SECONDARY MISSIONS OF THE SACRED LITURGY

Chapter VI: The Liturgy and Asceticism   55

Chapter VII: The Liturgy and Prayer   66

Chapter VIII: The Liturgy and Preaching   81

Chapter IX: The Liturgy and the Science of Theology   87

Conclusion   93

Preface

Dom Lambert Beauduin preached the community retreat at Farnborough in 1915, the year following the publication of the original French edition of *Liturgy the Life of the Church*. At that time Saint Michael's Abbey was renowned for its liturgical scholarship. Founded from Solesmes by Abbot Delatte in 1895, Farnborough's Abbot Cabrol presided over a community of monks famous for their works on liturgical history, theology and practice: Doms Férotin, Wilmart, Baudot, Gâtard, Gougaud, Villecourt, Leclercq, Cottineau, Steuart and Wesseling. Clearly this was a context and a community in which Dom Beauduin felt at home, for he was to visit Farnborough again in subsequent years.

The Sacred Liturgy is the fabric of the monastic life of our present-day community. The daily round of liturgical prayer, the performance of the ceremonies of the Liturgy as fully and as reverently as possible, the beauty of the chant, the pregnant texts of the feasts and seasons of the liturgical year, all leave their mark, not primarily on the intellect, but on the soul and on the heart. Liturgy is, indeed, the life of the monk.

Dom Beauduin's title reminds us that the Sacred Liturgy is also the life of the whole Church. Yet people of our day, most especially the young, often find contemporary liturgical celebrations lacking. They do not find the life the Liturgy offers. Their yearning for that sense of mystery, of beauty, of transcendence, their need for silence and for an experience of the numinous which is their right by virtue of their baptism is so often frustrated.

Though the liturgical problems of today are different to those of the beginning of the twentieth century when Dom Beauduin wrote this little book, the solution is similar: the whole Church must once again live and breathe the Church's Liturgy.

Today, as voices, from Cardinal Ratzinger down, call for a renewal of the classical Liturgical Movement in our time, Saint Michael's Abbey seeks once again to make a contribution –

somewhat more modest than that of our forebears – to the study of the Sacred Liturgy, and to this renewal.

One cannot drink from a spring unless that spring is accessible. Our new edition of *Liturgy the Life of the Church*, a classic of the Liturgical Movement and a classic of liturgical spirituality, is published precisely to facilitate that return to the sources without which future liturgical developments will lack the necessary foundation.

It is a pleasure, also, to have the opportunity to pay tribute to Dom Beauduin, an old friend of our community, and to rekindle the Farnborough Benedictine tradition of Dom Delatte, of Dom Cabrol, and of their communities.

Dom Cuthbert Brogan

Introduction

In 1906, a thirty three-year-old diocesan priest, Octave Beauduin, received the Benedictine habit and the religious name Lambert in the Abbey of Mont-César, Belgium. Here, he "discovered the Liturgy...during his noviciate: in the celebration of the divine office and the Mass with [the] young, small community."[1]

His pastoral experience and this discovery prompted Beauduin to submit a report, "De Promovenda Sacra Liturgia," to the General Chapter of the Beuronese Benedictine Congregation in July 1909.[2] The following September he articulated his convictions in a communication to the Catholic Conference at Malines. "This extraordinary man appealed courageously for a renewal of the liturgical life of the Church."[3] His paper "La vraie prière de l'Église"[4] earned the patronage of Cardinal Mercier, and the support of his hearers. The ideas presented in the 1909 paper were developed and published in 1914 as *La Piété de L'Église*, of which the present volume is a translation.

Louis Bouyer argues that Beauduin "augmented" the liturgical inheritance of Dom Guéranger, founder of the Abbey of Solesmes, "by the discovery of a most important principle:"

> That we must not try to provide an artificial congregation to take part in an antiquarian Liturgy, but rather to prepare the actual congregations of the Church today to take part in the truly traditional Liturgy rightly understood.[5]

---

[1] Bernard Botte, O.S.B., John Sullivan, trans., *From Silence to Participation: An Insider's View of Liturgical Renewal*, Pastoral Press, Washington DC 1988, p. 15.
[2] Cf. André Haquin, *Dom Lambert Beauduin et le Renouveau Liturgique*, Duculot, Gembloux 1970, pp. 234-237.
[3] Theodor Klauser, John Halliburton, trans., *A Short History of Western Liturgy*, second edition, Oxford University Press, Oxford 1979, p. 122.
[4] Cf. Haquin, op. cit., pp. 238-241.
[5] Louis Bouyer, Cong. Orat., *Life and Liturgy*, Sheed & Ward, London 1956 pp. 14-15.

Indeed, as one of Beauduin's confrères recalls:

> The Liturgical Movement, at its beginning, was not a reformist movement. Dom Beauduin knew very well that there were some cobwebs on that venerable monument called Liturgy. One day or another these would have to be dusted away. But he did not consider this as essential and, at any rate, it was not his business...He regarded the Liturgy as a traditional given which we first of all had to try to understand.[6]

We ought to be clear: in its origins, the Liturgical Movement did not aim to create oases of medieval liturgical splendour, nor did it seek to refashion the liturgical rites to achieve a so-called "pastoral" reform. Rather, it sought to nourish everyday Christian life by *participation of the mind and of the heart in the received Liturgy* wherever it was celebrated. It sought to awaken peoples' consciousness, including that of the clergy, to the Church's traditional spiritual treasury, the Sacred Liturgy.

Almost one hundred years and innumerable ritual reforms later, few would deny that this crucial goal is still to be realised. In part this may be said to be because the Liturgical Movement became distracted from its original aims.

This new edition[7] of Beauduin's small yet seminal volume places before us once again the vision of the Father of the twentieth century Liturgical Movement. May the Church of the twenty-first century rediscover its truth and work for its realisation, that the true pastoral benefits foreseen by Dom Beauduin may be enjoyed.

Br Alcuin Reid

---

[6] Botte, op. cit., pp. 22-23.
[7] This edition alters Dom Virgil Michel's translation but slightly, and only to render the author's meaning clear today. References have been added or expanded to assist further study.

PART ONE

THE RESTORATION OF THE SACRED LITURGY

Chapter I

The Fundamental Principle

The superabundant source of all supernatural life is the sacerdotal power of the High Priest of the New Covenant.

But this sanctifying power Jesus Christ does not exercise here below except through the ministry of a *visible sacerdotal hierarchy*.

Hence close union with this hierarchy in the exercise of its priesthood is for *every* Christian and Catholic soul the authentic mode of union with the priesthood of Jesus Christ, and consequently the primary and indispensable source of supernatural life.

The truth expressed in the second statement above is the keystone of the arch of every Catholic edifice. This cannot be insisted upon too strongly. Universal Teacher and King of all times, Christ has transmitted all His power of teaching and of spiritual government to His visible hierarchy. Grand as this truth is, there is one still more sublime: The Eternal Priest has communicated to this hierarchy the very energies of His sanctifying power; *through it he realises the sanctification of the new humanity.*

Hence there is in our midst, in the spiritual society of which we are members, a visible organism enriched by the priesthood of Jesus Christ, whose supernatural function it is to lead Christian souls to live superabundantly the life of God. Undoubtedly the immediate action of God upon souls is not restricted by this new dispensation. But the soul that is desirous of living under the sanctifying influence of Christ — and is not that the intense desire of every interior soul? — will have nothing so much at heart as the maintenance of an intimate and continuous contact with the *priestly acts* of the visible hierarchy.

What are these priestly and hierarchical acts, the primary and indispensable source of the Christian life?

From what has been said above, the answer should be readily found. It is the sanctifying mission of the Catholic hierarchy *(munus ministerii* — the mission of the ministry) to make of us living and holy oblations, offered daily unto the glory of the Father, in union with the unique sacrifice of Jesus Christ — a mission that is destined to extend all the divine energies of the eternal priesthood unto all generations.

Conscious of the primary importance of this mission, and solicitous of giving it full efficacy, the hierarchy has organised here below a sublime group of sacred functions in which the priesthood of Christ finds its full expression. This group of functions embraces every priestly act of the visible hierarchy. It is, in a word, the *Liturgy*. What a wonderful work when viewed in all its full import! Let us describe it briefly.

Central in it, dominating and unifying all the rest, is the Eucharistic Sacrifice, by virtue of which the faithful assembled in brotherly love daily assimilate to themselves the work of the Redemption. In this work the priestly power does not leave them to their own devices. A series of pious readings, of praises, of supplications, of rites and chants, inculcate the supreme importance of the great Mystery, and place it within the grasp of their souls. From the altar, the centre of the supernatural life, radiate the other sacraments, which the priestly power dispenses to them by means of various acts of worship.

Centring around this hearth of divine life is the Divine Office, which establishes an uninterrupted exchange of praise and blessings between heaven and earth, associates the Christian people, through their priests, with the Liturgy of eternity, and diffuses the blessings of the morning sacrifice over all the hours of day and night.

Next to the sacraments, the mysteries of the life of our divine Saviour are destined for the sanctification of men. Hence the priestly power of the Church, by means of the liturgical cycle, revives in our mind the great events of the Gospels, and at every liturgical season presents, so to speak, a new aspect of the life of the divine Saviour.

In order to intensify this sanctifying action in souls, the sacred hierarchy groups the people of God in families, or parishes, and confides the care of these to co-operators in its priesthood. These families each have their own *central hearth,* "house of God and gate of heaven," where everything, from vestibule to apse, from floor to roof, speaks of holy purifications and anointings. They all have *their priest*, who "offers, blesses, presides, instructs and baptises;" *their holy meetings*, where all the brethren transform themselves into Christ through the action of the visible priesthood; their patron saints, their feasts, their anniversaries of joy and of sorrow! i.e., their parish life, the soul of which is the Liturgy, the common source of supernatural and hierarchical life.

Finally, inferior in rank, but also of great importance, are the many sacramentals, by means of which the priestly powers communicate a sacred character to the very world in which the brothers of Christ dwell. Blessed by the hand of the ministers of Christ, our natural life loses its profane character and is permeated by the supernatural. Places, times, individuals, dwellings, elements, years, days and hours — all, even our food and our sleep, are blessed and in some way share with us the supernatural economy. Being "new creatures," the members of the risen Christ are placed by the creative priesthood of the Church into an anticipated springtime of eternal glory.

Such, viewed in its entirety, is the wonderful sanctifying activity of the visible priesthood of Jesus Christ, which everywhere and at all periods of time extends its supernatural influence over the whole Christian world. To designate it more exactly still, it is the totality of acts performed at the instance of the priests according to the fixed formulas of the liturgical books.

The traditional language of the Church expresses it by one word: the *Liturgy*.

It is impossible, therefore, to overemphasise the fact that souls seeking God must associate themselves as intimately and as frequently as possible with all the manifestations of the hierarchical priestly life which has just been described, and which places them directly under the influence of the priesthood of Jesus Christ Himself.

That is the primary law of the sanctity of souls. For all alike, wise and ignorant, infants and adults, lay and religious, Christians of the first and Christians of the twentieth century, leaders of an active or of a contemplative life, for *all the faithful of the Church without exception,* the greatest possible active and frequent participation in the priestly life of the visible hierarchy, according to the manner prescribed in the liturgical canons, is the *normal and infallible path* to a solid piety that is sane, abundant, and truly Catholic, that makes them children of their holy Mother the Church in the fullest sense of this ancient and truly Christian phrase.

From this, one can readily understand the profound reason for the positive command of the Church, which imposes on all her children a minimum participation in the acts of the Liturgy, and on her consecrated ministers an obligation that is more extensive. It is this: that supernatural life languishes and dies outside the range of action of the priesthood of Christ. Participation can undoubtedly be reduced to a strict minimum without sin, but souls truly desirous of the life divine will tend to do just the contrary.

We cannot refrain from repeating: there exists here below the authentic and official institution in which the priesthood of Christ receives its full supernatural expansion. In all places, at all hours, this sublime array of sanctifying actions, codified in the collection of liturgical books, is placed within reach of the faithful. It is a grand stream of graces flowing continuously. The more souls come to it to refresh themselves, the more will they live the life of God.

The great restorer of all things in Jesus Christ, Saint Pius X, commenced his work with the following declaration that has inspired all our words:

> Filled as we are with a most ardent desire to see the true Christian spirit flourish in every respect and be preserved by all the faithful, we deem it necessary to provide before aught else for the sanctity and dignity of the temple, in which the faithful assemble for no other object than that of acquiring this spirit from its primary and indispensable source, which is the active participation in the most holy mysteries and in the public and solemn prayer of the Church *(Motu proprio "Tra le sollecitudini"* of Nov. 22, 1903[1]).

---

[1] Cf. C. Braga & A. Bugnini, eds., *Documenta Ad Instaurationem Liturgicam Spectantia 1903-1963*, Centro Liturgico Vincenziano, Rome, 2000, pp. 12-27; ET: R. Kevin Seasolz, *The New Liturgy: A Documentation 1903 - 1965*, Herder, New York 1966 pp. 3-10.

An important conclusion springs from this principle. The whole priestly influence is exercised on the members of the Church *only* by means of sensible, *authentic* forms, which are its vehicle. Formulas, readings, chants, rites, material elements, in short, all the externals of the Liturgy, are *indispensable* for sharing in the thoughts, the teachings, the acts of adoration, the sentiments, the graces which Christ and His visible priesthood destine for us. Hence, to minimise this visible contact under the pretext that the soul can then better achieve something interior, or that invisible communion suffices, is at the same time to diminish the priestly influence of the hierarchy and consequently the action of Christ in our souls.

If we should look at the supernatural activity of the soul only from the psychological point of view, we could limit the function of the sensory appeal entirely to the facilitation of mental prayer, and we could suppress or eliminate the senses if they became useless or harmful to this purpose. But we shall see further on that liturgical piety, with the wisdom of discretion, safeguards and greatly fosters this form of prayer.

In the Catholic economy of the supernatural life the activities of the senses have a higher purpose. They are the *necessary* channels of the thought and life of the Church, of Christ, of God. To depreciate ritual piety because it is not purely mental, to diminish one's participation in liturgical acts under the pretext of fostering a more interior life, is to withdraw oneself just to that extent also from the sanctifying action of the Church, to isolate oneself from the adoration and prayer of the Spouse of Christ, to lessen the influence of the priesthood of our Lord upon the soul.

Let us sing, then; let us lend our ears, open our eyes, unite ourselves completely to the priestly acts according to all the demands of the ritual; let us participate freely in all the functions of parochial life, assimilate all the riches of the liturgical texts, surrender ourselves to the action of our holy Church, in a word, *live the mystery of the hierarchy*, whatever may be our degree of interior prayer, our private method, or our attraction for solitude. It is thus that we shall find the manna of the desert, the family table, the embrace of our Mother Church, nay, Jesus Himself, God.

Liturgical piety derives its transcendent character above all from what we can call its *hierarchical character*. It procures the full sanctifying influence of the visible priesthood of the mystical body of Jesus Christ for the members of this body. The life of God is in Christ; the life of Christ is in the hierarchy of the Church. The hierarchy realises this life in souls by its priestly power; and this priestly power is exercised in the authentic acts performed according to the liturgical books: Missal, Breviary, Ritual, Ceremonial of the Bishops, Pontifical, Martyrology. *These acts are therefore the primary and indispensable source of true Catholic piety.*

We are, therefore, not making any appeal at present to the doctrinal, psychological, pedagogical, popular, or aesthetic aspects of the Liturgy. Also from these points of view, as we shall see, the supremacy of the Liturgy is incontestable. Even if that were not the case, however, the Liturgy would ever preserve its full and complete primacy; for it is the very piety of our holy Mother, the Roman Catholic Church. *"Adhaereat lingua mea faucibus meis, si non meminero tui Jerusalem:* Let my tongue cleave to my jaws if I do not remember thee, O Jerusalem!" (Ps. 136:6.)

Chapter II

The Present Condition: the Nature of the Evil

Active participation in the liturgical life of the Church is a capital factor in the supernatural life of the Christian. We found the evidence thereof in the organic life of the Church.

Is it necessary, on the other hand, to prove the existence of almost complete ignorance or apathy among the faithful in regard to liturgical worship? That matter is too evident, and we shall not stop to describe it.

The position which sacrifice should hold in religion and in the life of the faithful; the understanding and love of holy Mass; filial and supernatural confidence in the hierarchy; the importance of the parish High Mass and of all collective manifestations of the Christian life; a faith, full of confidence and respect, in the rites of the sacraments and the sacramentals; the sanctification of the day of the Lord; the pious and collective celebration of the great events of the liturgical cycle; the life of our Lord, of the Virgin Mother, of the Saints, lived by *the whole Christian people* through the liturgical feasts; the spirit of penitence inculcated by Lent; knowledge of the Psalms, the Gospels, the Acts of the Apostles, the Epistles, the Sacred Scriptures in general, which form the fabric of the liturgical books; the cult of the dead, to which the Liturgy of the Church has given so Christian a character; the many wholesome practices which formerly transmitted to family and social life the echo of the piety of the Church, and conserved in human society, now secularised, a deeply religious character; in a word, this constant affirmation of supernatural realities, which created a collective Catholic mentality and proclaimed here below the rights of the Most Holy Trinity — all these immense realities have lost much of their sanctifying action. It is not necessary to give any proofs here or to inquire into the causes. The fact can be observed by all, since it is a matter of general experience. And, as to the problem, every sincere Catholic will find in his personal experience, in the memory of his years of study, of his parochial life, his spiritual retreats, his reading, in all his religious life, the indications of a solution that is unerring.

In commencing this examination of conscience, let us not be satisfied with superficial statements; and let us not confuse the accessory aspects with the essential purpose of the Liturgy.

For many casual observers, a liturgical restoration may mean nothing but an interesting manifestation of the contemporary artistic and idealistic reawakening, and of the sympathetic curiosity which history and sacred rites arouse among so many — a pious dilettantism, a capricious turn for the archaic, which haunts certain minds that are enthralled by ancient forms. For them there is only question of the artistic touch in the paintings and furniture of religious edifices. The interest is almost wholly aesthetic. Undoubtedly we can well encourage this legitimate tendency. But it is nevertheless very secondary. In accentuating it too exclusively, there is great danger of fostering the notion that the Liturgy is without ascetic import and can engender nothing but a sentimental and artistic piety in which the intelligence and the efficient activity of the soul abdicate in favour of a vague impressionism and of fleeting and sterile emotions. Saint Pius X in his liturgical reform did not speak as archaeologist or artist, but as the *Vicar of the Eternal Priest.*

It would likewise be an odd limitation of the spirit of the Liturgical Movement, to see in it primarily a matter of mere ceremonies. Surely, care for detailed exactness and for reverence in the performance of liturgical acts is eminently priestly, and a source of edification to the faithful. Following the example of God Himself in the Old Law, the Church does not disdain to concern herself with all the details of the ritual. The minor prescriptions regarding the number of candles on the altar, the quality of the incense, the vestments of the acolytes, and so many others, that excite the sarcasm of unbelievers — all are worthy of our respect. But they form only one element of the Liturgy. Looked at exclusively from their point of view, the Liturgy can have only the value of external formality — hence also the discredit which has so undeservedly been its lot. What would we say of a critic who in the sermons of Bossuet sought for nothing but the application of dictionary and syntax rules?

We shall perhaps surprise more than one reader by saying that, in order to remedy the evil from which the faithful of our generation are suffering in regard to the Liturgy, it will not suffice to initiate them into the ritual formulas and ceremonies, into the dogmatic and symbolical meanings of the latter, and into their historical origin. This knowledge is undoubtedly necessary for rendering the meaning of the Sunday, or the participation in the mysteries and other functions of the Church, properly intelligible, instructive, attractive, and fruitful. But the work of liturgical restoration is intended to combat an evil that lies deeper, to pursue its purpose more thoroughly.

The piety of the Christian people, and hence their actions and life, are not grounded sufficiently in the fundamental truths that constitute the soul of the Liturgy; that is, in the destiny of all things unto the glory of the Father, the Son, and the Holy Ghost; the necessary and universal contemplation of Jesus Christ; the central place of the Eucharistic Sacrifice in the Christian life; the mission of the hierarchy in regard to our union with God; the visible realisation of the Communion of Saints. All these truths, which find expression in every liturgical act, are asleep in men's souls; the faithful have lost consciousness of them. Let us change the routine and monotonous assistance at acts of worship into an active and intelligent participation; let us teach the faithful to pray and confess these truths in a body: and the Liturgy thus practised will insensibly arouse a slumbering faith and give new efficacy, both in prayer and action, to the latent energies of the baptised souls: "the true Christian spirit will flourish again and maintain itself among the faithful."

Utopia! Dream of another age! Undoubtedly the work will be arduous. People have for centuries ignored this traditional piety; it will take them a long time to re-learn it.

But Saint Pius X, taught by a half-century of active ministry, which was exercised in all ranks of the ecclesiastical hierarchy, the great pope of practical and pastoral initiative, affirmed, at the beginning of his glorious pontificate, his firm will to lead the faithful back to this "primary and indispensable source of the Christian spirit," and his efforts have been continued by his successors in the chair of Peter. It is the voice of Christ Himself that calls!

Chapter III

The Consequences of the Present Condition

1. Individualism. 2. Abandonment of Prayer. 3. Deviations of Piety. 4. The Secular Spirit. 5. Lack of Hierarchical Life.

We have seen the nature of the evil which Saint Pius X wished to remedy by means of the liturgical restoration. We shall now mention briefly the pernicious effects which the abandonment of the Liturgy produced in the mystical body of Christ.

1. INDIVIDUALISM

The Christian does not walk alone on the path of his pilgrimage. God desired other than that his adorers should go to Him individually, each for himself. There is nothing more contrary to the divine conception. Christ, in fashioning the visible organism which was to survive Him and to accomplish His work, wished to realise among men that unity of which He found the exemplar and model in God Himself: "That they may be one as we also are one!" (John 17:22)

Begun with the visible bonds of the Roman Church, this society prolongs and realises itself in eternity; it embraces all souls sanctified by Jesus Christ, our elder Brother. Between the Church of heaven and the Church of earth there exists an intimate union which shall one day become perfect. This union manifests, nourishes, and develops itself by a common participation in spiritual goods, by the communication of merits and individual goods, by a continual exchange of prayers offered to God for the welfare and spiritual progress of each member and for the increasing prosperity of the entire body.

The Catholic is therefore, by definition, *a member of a visible organism*. There is no doubt, as we shall see later, that he preserves his own activity and personal responsibility. But the elements of knowledge and of life come to him from a single source, Jesus Christ, through visible communion with the Church.

Religious individualism is, then, quite contrary to the conception of Catholicism.

Evidently there can be no question among the faithful of an individualism that reaches into doctrinal teaching, morals, discipline, and the sacramental life. A soul that isolates itself on these essential points ceases to be Catholic.

An essential unity on these points, however, does not suffice for souls that are truly Catholic; they desire that this union of minds and hearts be affirmed and cemented by perfect community of worship. To pray alone, to make our supernatural life an individual affair between ourselves and God, instead of uniting ourselves heart and voice to the prayer of our brethren and of the celebrating priest, who in his priestly function personifies the entire Church united to its head, Jesus Christ — what is this but *deforming in ourselves the Catholic mentality* and refusing to collaborate in a common work?

Hence, from the first centuries to our own day, the Church has ever given to all her prayer a profoundly and essentially collective character. By means of living the Liturgy wholeheartedly, Christians become more and more conscious of their supernatural fraternity, of their union in the mystical body of Christ. And this is the most powerful antidote against the individualism to which our natural egoism surrenders itself so readily. It can therefore be said in all truth that *whatever the Liturgy loses is gained by individualism.*

2. ABANDONMENT OF PRAYER

Many Christians no longer pray at all. This is the *inevitable* consequence of the neglect into which liturgical prayer has fallen. Undoubtedly, chosen souls can without guidance or training learn to preserve a spirit of intense prayer, provided, of course, they perform the essential liturgical acts. But how can *the ordinary people, the multitude of the faithful,* surrounded as they are by the tempestuous affairs of our time, burdened with the things of earth, acquire the wings necessary to raise themselves unaided to God? Our holy Mother Church does not abandon these less privileged children to their isolation and personal weakness. She has produced for them a social environment which will supply their individual deficiencies; namely, the liturgical gatherings properly so called.

At these assemblies, association multiplies the energies and the capacities of the individual, and creates a powerful atmosphere, which will carry along the more feeble. A collective soul permeates the entire assembly. The phenomenon of the psychology of crowds is pressed into the service of God. In the Liturgy everything is so disposed as to intensify this action: pomp of ceremonies, dramatic character of the sacred functions, dialogue between priest and faithful, collective singing. What invitations to prayer! What stimulating inspirations! What incitement towards God! Alas! This radiating warmth has deserted our liturgical assemblies; the people are cold in our churches; they are annoyed; they come as to a forced service, and are in a hurry to get away: the entire attitude denotes that their souls are elsewhere — they no longer pray.

It is necessary to restore the collective soul to the social environment created by the Church for prayer. If, while there is yet time, we reanimate this benumbed body, the liturgical assembly, the Christian people will return to prayer. After the example of our divine Lord, Saint Pius X has taught his disciples the secret of true prayer.

Above all, the more fervent souls among the faithful must not forget that it is an important social duty of charity for them to place their personal fervour at the service of this restoration of collective piety. It is they, especially, who by their zeal, their active participation in the singing, by the sacrifice of their individual preferences, must restore full vitality to the liturgical gatherings of the parish. This can well be called a spiritual work of mercy of the first order.

3. DEVIATIONS OF PIETY

The Liturgy is the school in which the Church teaches us to pray.

Outside this school, it is easy to deviate from the true method. Catholic prayer has its laws, which the Church applies with constant fidelity in her worship.

We have developed the three essential laws elsewhere. The Most Holy Trinity is the object of worship; Jesus Christ, and His mystical body through Him, are the subject rendering worship; the sacrifice of the Cross renewed in the Eucharist is its central act. These fundamental principles can be well expressed in a single formula: *The Church consecrates us daily to the glory of the Most Holy Trinity by means of the sacrifice of the Eucharist.* This primary notion of the Christian life must penetrate into the very depths of our souls and vivify our every action.

It is unquestionably true that for many of the faithful the dogma of the Most Holy Trinity, the universal mediation of Jesus Christ, the idea of the holy Sacrifice, are truths purely of the speculative order. Nevertheless, it is impossible to be resigned to this order of things. It is impossible that these fundamental treasures of the New Dispensation, instituted for the benefit of the humble and the lowly, should remain without an echo in their souls, in their relations with God, and in their Christian life. It is here precisely, that we place our finger on the true efficacy of the Liturgy. Through the latter the Church infuses these most essential truths insensibly into the hearts and the minds of her most humble servants, not by formulas but by acts.

Furthermore, Christian piety in isolating itself easily becomes fanciful, occupying itself with secondary practices to the detriment of a more substantial devotion. Hence we may find among Catholics, even those well instructed and well disposed, a confusion between devotion and devotionalism, while the anti-religious press finds therein a subject for pleasantries and for jibes, which are more or less justified and which throw discredit both upon religion in general and upon piety.

On March 28, 1914 the Holy See disapproved of a form of devotion, whose success was ephemeral, and offered to those seeking for new devotions the wise prescription of Blessed Pius IX:

> That all those faithful and those authors who torment their minds with subtleties on this subject and upon others of this

nature savouring of novelty, and who under the cover of piety try to promote, even by the founding of new periodicals, titles of extraordinary devotions, should be advised to abstain from their attempts, and to reflect on the danger there is of thus drawing the faithful into error, sometimes even on points of faith, and of exposing our religion to the sarcasm of our enemies, who use such occasions for railing at the purity of Catholic doctrine and at true piety.[1]

The charge, that liturgical piety is the enemy of private devotion, therefore rests on a misunderstanding. It is true that the former is, in this domain, traditional, discreet, even extremely reserved. The sickly desire that is ever in quest of pious novelties justly frightens the liturgical mentality. The latter is the enemy of all devotionalism, and glories in being that. But far from destroying traditional and authentic private devotions, it gives them an increase of vigour and strength. A stranger to all fashions and to all fads, imbued with sane doctrine, pure and unalloyed, broad and generous, the Liturgy, having become the principle food of the Christian soul, will transform its private devotion, give it a new impetus, a new intensity, while at the same time keeping it in its proper place.

4. THE SECULAR SPIRIT

Etudes recognised this spirit in the following words (Nov. 20, 1913, p. 450): "The liturgical apostolate offers the most efficacious antidote to the poison of the secular spirit, which creeps unconsciously into the hearts of our best people." To restrict religious life to the inner conscience and to consider it only as something secret and invisible, to suppress all religious acts completely in social and public life, to treat of God as the great Unknown of enlightened humanity — such is the anti-religious programme of the enemies of Christianity.

We are living in a social and political atmosphere that is saturated with this secular spirit. The latter tries to insinuate itself into Catholic life in many subtle and equivocal forms: tolerance,

---

[1] Cf. Braga & Bugnini, *Documenta*, pp. 153-154.

respect for opinions, religion discreet and reserved, piety in which the spirit plays a larger part than the rites: *"in spiritu et veritate oportet illum adorare:* they must adore him in spirit and in truth" (John 4:24) — and what not! How poorly the Liturgy is adapted to this impoverished Christianity, is evident enough. In the Liturgy we have professions of faith, collective prayers, obligatory gatherings of the faithful, public confession of adherence to the Church for all alike, an exuberant enthusiasm for the supernatural life.

It is not only the faithful whose faith is reanimated by the Liturgy. The indifferent, even the adversaries in spite of themselves, feel the influence of this externalised religious life. The grand cathedrals, inspired by the Liturgy and constructed for it, and rising in our public places; the towers, cupolas, spires, symbols of our faith, which catch the eye from a distance and dominate our public dwellings and our private residences; the chimes, which sing out; the processions that take place; the funeral cortèges that pray and hope; the joyful crowds that go in long files to the house of the Lord to celebrate our grand religious solemnities; the liturgical cycle, sending its rhythm into the civil life and imposing on the latter respect for its holy days — in a word, all the exterior manifestations that the Liturgy inspires, animates, and preserves, are a protest against this atheistic secularisation, and constitute in our midst *a constant affirmation of the supernatural and of the rights of God.*

It is impossible to deny the great religious import of a movement which, besides other things, proposes to develop among the people a strong love for, and an attachment to, the Christian life in its entirety.

Frequently the enemies of the Church have understood the extreme importance of public worship better than we have. The Roman emperors were not troubled about the purely private and individual practice of the Christian religion; what they forbade absolutely were the religious gatherings, the sacrifices offered in common, the collective prayers, in a word, liturgical piety. By his edict of 249 the Emperor Decius ordered all the inhabitants of his empire, without distinction of age or sex, to take themselves to the temple on an appointed day and to sacrifice there. He prescribed the three acts which each one was to perform: offering of incense, libations and, above all, partaking of the flesh of the victims. He understood correctly that the suppression of its collective worship would be a death-blow to the Christian religion. And all the persecutors of the Church down to our own day have used the same tactics.

Yes, the Liturgy is the constant and public confession of Jesus Christ by the Church herself. In remaining faithful to it we shall merit the promise of our divine Master: "Everyone that shall confess me before men, I will also confess him before My Father who is in heaven" (Matt. 10:32).

5. LACK OF HIERARCHICAL LIFE

The existence of a visible hierarchy of divine origin in the Church is a truth of which Christians are often not sufficiently conscious. We have said enough of this in Chapter I. The proper mission of this hierarchy, the mission for which it receives all its powers, is to minister the divine life to humanity: it is therefore essentially that of *a spiritual fatherhood, of a priesthood of inexhaustible fecundity.*

This true aspect of religious authority sometimes escapes our compromising mentalities. In the eyes of some, the power of the Sovereign Pontiff and of the bishops seems to be nothing but a vast administrative machinery placed over the spiritual life, an authentic ministry of worship, a spiritual police, a watchful guardian over dogma and morals. Reduced to this narrow angle, the eyes of a weakened faith no longer distinguish the spiritual fathers from the mere brethren of Christ. It then becomes difficult to realise that the interior soul, after having satisfied the essential demands of dogma, of discipline, and of worship, can still attain a further development of the spiritual life through the actions of the hierarchical power. Is not this a rather simple outlook and by far too elementary, one that in no way answers the needs of the chosen souls? There necessarily follows from it a falling off in the sentiments of respect, of filial confidence, of supernatural obedience — an effect that is plainly opposed to the greater vitality of the body of Christ. This it is that the saintly Pius X had deplored in such severe terms. Liturgical piety, properly understood, is the best weapon for combating this evil. We have already said that it places us under the active influence of the priestly power of the Church. In it the hierarchy exercises its spiritual fatherhood; and the faithful, nourished at the family table under the presidency of the head of the family, draw thence the filial respect, the loving obedience, the *esprit de corps* which constitute their strength.

Do we reflect on this truth sufficiently? The liturgical books that day by day regulate our sacrifices, our adoration, and our prayers, draw all their powers of praise, of intercession, and of sanctity, from the fact that they are given to us by the supreme head of the hierarchy. That they have come to us from Saint Leo, Saint Gelasius, Saint Gregory, is of little importance for the moment. Their transcendent and incomparable title in the eyes of the Father who is in heaven, and in the eyes of the faithful, is that they form the great prayer presided over by the Vicar of Jesus Christ, the reigning Pontiff. Every time that the faithful in the Catholic world associate themselves with the holy Mass, the Divine Office, the solemnities of the liturgical cycle, with any liturgical act, they share in the adoration and the prayer of the Supreme Pontiff and through him of the entire Church; they are the children that nourish themselves at the table of our common parent, the Holy Father.

If all the faithful would daily live this liturgical piety, which can in all truth be called *filial piety,* would not the authority of our common father be holy and sacred under all circumstances, and would not the supreme wish that our Lord formulated in His priestly prayer be realised: *that they be one as we also are one?*

As a school of respect for, and attachment to, the supreme head of the visible hierarchy, the Liturgy also greatly strengthens the bonds of every diocesan church. The bishop there appears as the father and pontiff of his church, whether he personally performs the Liturgy in his cathedral, his mother-church, or whether he does so through his co-operators in the parishes, his daughter churches. We have already emphasised these different aspects of the Liturgy, and shall not repeat them here. A word in conclusion will suffice.

To pray with the Vicar of Jesus Christ, with his bishop, with his priest; to associate oneself actively with the hierarchy in

Part One: The Restoration of the Sacred Liturgy

the offering of the Sacrifice, in the recitation of the Office at least on Sundays; to participate extensively in the parochial life; in short, to develop a hierarchical piety — all this will serve to strengthen the necessary bonds of subordination and attachment, which should exist between *the priesthood and the Christian people*. If, then, among so many crises in life there comes also a crisis of obedience, it is a matter of certainty that the Christian soul, united to the life and the thought of the Church by means of the Liturgy, by reason of spiritual habits long grown dear, will find easy and sure guidance in a sense of filial obedience that is both complete and sincere.

Chapter IV

The Advantages of Liturgical Piety

1. The Christian, a Member of the Church. 2. Attachment to the Church of Rome. 3. Social Sense of Catholicism. 4. Realisation of the Sacramental Riches. 5. Method of Instruction. 6. Social Influence. 7. Apologetic Value.

The Liturgy comprises the priestly acts of the hierarchy. This is the reason for its transcendence, the basis of all its power, its primary title to the esteem of all the faithful. Even apart from this value, which comes to it from Christ through the hierarchy, it possesses intrinsic qualities, multiple riches, with which, under the guidance of the Holy Ghost, the Church could not but endow it. Hence the numerous advantages to those who endeavour to utilise all its resources, advantages which are secondary in regard to the above primary aspect, but which nevertheless contribute largely to the full development of a Catholic life. We shall indicate a few of them briefly.

1. THE CHRISTIAN A MEMBER OF THE CHURCH

The members must have the same life as the body of which they are parts. The laws which regulate the activities of the body must be also their laws. This is a necessary condition of order, of harmony, of peace.

As a true member, the Catholic ought to adapt himself, unite himself as intimately as possible, to the mystical body of Christ. The state of his soul, his activity, his mentality, his whole moral being, should be modelled on the intimate nature of the Church, should vibrate with the very pulse-beat of the Church. He must be not only *in* the Church, but *of* the Church, live from the fullness of her life, be cast in the same mould.

Now the Church, her intimate life, her thought, her aspirations, her traditions, her entire soul, are unfolded precisely in her prayer. The latter has sprung spontaneously from her nature; it contains all her essential traits.

The Christian, therefore, in faithfully living the Liturgy, develops in himself the life of the Church.

And the result is remarkable indeed. We cannot be content with a mere general statement here, but shall give a brief outline of the essential traits of the Catholic Church, in order to see how well they are exemplified in the Liturgy.

The essential elements of the Church can be put down as five: the Church is the universal society (first two elements) founded by Christ (third element) for the sanctification (fourth element) of men (fifth element). The five elements are found also in her official worship.

A. THE SOCIAL CHARACTER OF THE LITURGY

Dogmatic foundation. The Church of Christ is essentially a visible society having a visible hierarchy as its head.

Realisation in the Liturgy. From this the first characteristics of the Church's worship naturally follow. This worship is: 1. *Collective*, being the worship not of an individual but of a collective body. 2. *Hierarchical*. In order to be a responsible enactment of the religious society, these collective acts must be performed in its name by those properly delegated, or under the presidency of those who officially impersonate the entire body. This condition follows from the very notion of society. Without it the worship would be anarchic; worship of the Church necessarily means hierarchical worship. 3. *Externalised*. On the other hand, since no communication can exist between men except by means of the senses, the interior worship of the individual members can be fused into a common prayer of the entire Church only if vested in a sensible form. In order to complete and to socialise the interior element of the worship, an external element must be added. Hence the worship of the Church is of necessity also external. 4. *Official*. Finally, these sensible, forms whether they be natural or artificial, must have legal recognition; they must be established by the proper authority. The worship of the Church is therefore necessarily also official (hence the official liturgical books).

B. UNIVERSAL CHARACTER OF THE LITURGY

Dogmatic Foundation. There is but one true Church, which shall endure unto the end of time, and in which all generations of people can find the complete redemption of Jesus Christ.

Realisation in the Liturgy. From this fact we get a second series of characteristics in the Liturgy. Above all the Liturgy is: 1. *One.* Unity of belief, of discipline, of common fellowship, must necessarily show itself in worship; and despite certain divergences the Liturgy is fundamentally, profoundly *one*. 2. *Traditional.* This unity must be realised also in point of time. The Church of today is the Church of all times and of all peoples; hence her Liturgy is traditional. This characteristic is so important that it receives precedence over that of uniformity, as is seen in the preservation of the Oriental rites. 3. *Living.* The former characteristic does not make of the Liturgy a fossilised antique, a museum curiosity. The Liturgy *lives* and unfolds itself also today and, because universal, is of the twentieth century as well as of the first. It lives and follows the dogmatic and organic developments of the Church herself.

C. CHRISTIAN CHARACTER OF THE LITURGY

Dogmatic Foundation. The Church is Christ Himself continuing through the centuries with all His teachings and His merits and His work. "As the Father hath sent me, I also send you" (John 20, 21). But Christ can be viewed in His three stages: *Christ yesterday and today and in all eternity.* He consummates the Old Testament, He consummates the New, He consummates all eternity.

Realisation in the Liturgy. The Liturgy is: 1. *Judaic.* It accords full value to the Old Testament and has borrowed much from Hebrew worship. 2. *Evangelical.* It gives life, above all, to the New Testament. The liturgical cycle makes us, as it were, contemporaries of Christ. The teachings, the parables of our Lord, are constantly placed before us in its rites and formulas. 3. *Prefiguring eternity.* Christ is now in heaven and, it is there that the true Liturgy is consummated. Saint John has given us some echoes thereof: *"In sublime altare tuum, in conspectu divinæ majestatis tuæ:* In Thy altar on High, in the sight of Thy divine Majesty" (cf. Apoc. 8:2f.).

D. SANCTIFYING CHARACTER OF THE LITURGY

Dogmatic Foundation. The Church has received from Christ the *munus ministerii,* the duty of ministering, for the purpose of sanctifying all mankind and of helping it to glorify the Most Holy Trinity here below and in eternity.

Realisation in the Liturgy. The aim of the Liturgy, as Saint Pius X said, is twofold: to glorify God and to sanctify men. In regard to the first of these functions the Liturgy is 1. *Latreutical,* i.e., rendering divine worship. Adoration of God, with all the attitudes of soul included therein, predominates in the worship of the Church; whereas private devotion easily becomes too full of self-interest. In regard to the sanctification of men the Liturgy is: 2. *Didactic.* For without faith holiness is impossible. The Liturgy teaches all the doctrines of Christ with incomparable force. It is finally: 3. *Sanctifying.* It produces grace through the sacraments, constantly begging it of God with all the power of intercession of the Church; and it disposes us to receive the sacraments with the sentiments of faith, of confidence, and of compunction that it excites in our souls.

E. HUMAN CHARACTER OF THE LITURGY

Theological Foundation. Both in the supernatural and in the natural order it is a law that God has made unto Himself, to dispense His gifts to men through the mediation of men themselves. This is the very keystone of the vault of the entire ecclesiastical edifice. The procedure in the relations of the supernatural order must therefore be modelled on that found in human nature, as Christ Himself demonstrated in all His work.

Realisation in the Liturgy. The Liturgy is always: 1. *Psychological.* The forms of worship of the Church are faithful to this principle, which is ever that of sound psychology: *nihil in intellectu quod non fuerit prius in sensu*.[1] For this reason the Liturgy is also largely: 2. *Symbolic*. The symbolism must be reasonable, suited to the occasion and, above all, biblical. It is finally: 3. *Aesthetic*. The Church, knowing the power of artistic action and expression, has always employed all the art in her worship.

This theological analysis plainly shows the resources which the faithful will find in the Liturgy if the latter is lived; resources that will develop more and more their *ecclesiastical* soul (in the profoundest and most practical sense of this word), that is, a soul penetrated with a sincere and effective sense of orthodoxy, of devotion to the true interests of the Church, of loyal and affectionate submission to the directions of ecclesiastical authority.

It is hardly necessary to remark that we do not claim these advantages as the exclusive monopoly of liturgical piety. But we do claim that the latter is the indispensable means of creating and maintaining this mentality *in the mass of the Christian people*, of infusing this truly Catholic spirit not *only into a choice number of souls, but into the whole society of the faithful*, of creating *a Christianity and not merely Christians*.

Again, we do not mean to impugn in any way the perfect orthodoxy of those who no not accord to the Liturgy the preponderant place in the spiritual life that we have assigned it. The Church has imposed on all her children a minimum of participation in her Liturgy. In the fulfilment of this precept according to the demands, or better the condescension, of the moralists, the law has indeed been satisfied. But we are here not seeking the strict minimum requirement; we are seeking *the method that procures the maximum of Catholic life*, that not merely places us *in* the Church, but makes us to be *of* the Church. In order to become established in a new country to enjoy all the rights of a citizen, it is not necessary to be *of* that particular country. It is necessary, however, to know and to speak its language, to mingle day and night in its life, which is different from that of other countries, to acquire its customs, frequent its

---

[1] An adage in scholastic philosophy; and accepted generally by others also. It expresses the fact that all our human knowledge comes naturally to our minds through the channels of our senses.

gatherings, and thus gradually to share its tastes, its tendencies, its mentality, as a result of the daily contact which creates the mysterious and profound influence of social environment. Thus alone can a foreigner become truly one with the citizens of his new country. It is not sufficient, therefore, to fulfil perfectly the formalities required by law; without daily living contact, the foreigner would always remain a foreigner. He could, undoubtedly, find a partial remedy in the study of the laws and institutions of his adopted country, by reading various books explaining its life and ideals. But apart from the fact that this method of assimilation is not within the capacity of most people, it would not prevent the display of certain mannerisms, which betray the poorly disguised foreigner.

Where, then, shall we, as members of the Church, associate ourselves with the manifestations of the daily normal, natural life of adoration and prayer of this holy society, to which we wish to belong in body and soul? Where are its gatherings held? Where do we experience contact with our fellow citizens of heaven and earth? Where does this society speak its own language, the language of its Liturgy, vehicle of all its thoughts, its traditions, its soul? Where, in the strictest sense of the term, can we become *citizens of the city of God?*

2. ATTACHMENT TO THE CHURCH OF ROME

The intelligent and loving frequenting of the Liturgy increases and strengthens the Catholic spirit also for another most special reason: it makes us live in the capital of the Christian world. By means of the Church's Liturgy we are made citizens of the Eternal City. Dom Cabrol, in a series of conferences held at the 1912 Maredsous "Liturgical Week"[2] on the stations of Rome,[3] the

---

[2] Cf. *Cours et Conférences de la Semaine Liturgique de Maredsous 19-24 Août 1912*, Abbaye de Maredsous, Maredsous 1913.
[3] The Stations of Rome are the different churches at which the Roman people and clergy gathered for the common celebration of the great Sundays and feasts. The Liturgy often found its inspiration in circumstances connected with the special church of the day. The Roman missal today still mentions the special station churches of these occasions. Cf. *Catholic Encyclopaedia*, "Station Days."

grand basilicas, and the liturgical cycle of the Roman feasts, showed what great benefit we can derive from the Liturgy in regard to this sentiment, which is so characteristically Catholic. After mentioning the great monuments of Rome, he said:

> This is our history, the history of our Christian origins, the epic of the Rock. All these monuments speak to our heart and to our faith. Rome has become a second capital for us. I should like to point out to you the bonds that connect these archaeological monuments with the Liturgy. The Roman Liturgy is there realised in the concrete; it was a local liturgy there before becoming the Liturgy of the Latin world. I should also like to point out that you, friends and confreres, with your missal and breviary, and you, gentlemen of the laity, with your parish manuals,[4] have to hand all the elements of this history; and I should like to reassure you that this study gives additional interest to those books, and at the same time to the Liturgy.

By means of the Liturgy, well understood and lived daily, Rome should occupy in the love and the worship of Catholics the place that Jerusalem occupied in the love and the worship of the children of Israel. *"Stantes erant pedes nostri in atriis tuis Jerusalem:* Our feet were standing in thy courts, O Jerusalem" (Ps. 122:2). We frequently perform this pilgrimage *ad limina,* to Rome, by understanding and living the Roman Liturgy. The Stations in the great basilicas, which inspire so many liturgical texts, the cult of all the martyrs of the persecutions, the origin of rites and formulas, all attach us to the Mother Church, mistress of all.

Furthermore, devotion to the liturgical cause, in uniting us to the Roman Church, also introduces us into the thought and the desires of the saintly liturgist, Pius X, and of his successors. We cannot here recount all the liturgical acts of these pontificates. It will suffice to quote the authoritative words by which Cardinal Mercier summed up the great significance of every action of the restorer of all things in Christ:

---

[4]*"Paroissien"* — a manual (missal) for the laity, containing the general liturgical prayers of parish services, Masses, Vespers, prayers for the day, blessings, etc.

Part One: The Restoration of the Sacred Liturgy

When our Holy Father, Pius X, speaks, gives an order, or simply lets his wishes be divined, all of us, faithful, clergy, and bishops, must submit with the same respectful docility as if our divine Saviour, come back to earth, were Himself explaining His Gospel to us. Now you can readily note, if you will, that all the acts, all the deeds of our well-beloved Pope have a double object: to strengthen the bonds of the hierarchy by consolidating authority, and to revivify baptised souls by leading them back to the sources of supernatural life (Address to his clergy, January 28, 1914).

The work of Saint Pius X has been faithfully continued by his successors. All that we have so far said indicates, therefore, that the restoration of the Liturgy ever answers the most intimate desires of the head of the Catholic hierarchy.

3. SOCIAL SENSE OF CATHOLICISM

This social sense comprises three elements: (1) Necessity of a *collective* life (as opposed to the religious individualism of a Sabatier); (2) of a collective life instituted and maintained *from without* by the supernatural action of a legitimate authority (as opposed to the immanence of the Modernists); (3) and rendered *visible* by external action: faith professed, signs conferred, exterior communion, etc. (as opposed to the invisible church of the Protestants). The Catholic Liturgy bears the impress of this triple character in all its manifestations. It is *collective,* for by it all live collectively the same spirituality, that of the Church; it is *hierarchical,* for with its doctrines, its rites, and its spirit, it comes from the Roman Church; it is *visible,* for all of it is expressed in symbols and formulas. Hence the method of piety inculcated in us by the Liturgy develops in us *the social sense of Catholicism* and furnishes us with the most powerful antidote against modern errors.

Minds versed in theological science, undoubtedly possess other equally efficacious means of fortifying themselves against the errors of today. But the *ordinary faithful,* desirous of a more intense interior life, cannot safeguard himself sufficiently against the many captious illusions of subjectivism and illuminism without the constant guidance of the visible hierarchical piety. Speaking of these errors in his famous work on the priestly vocation *(La Vocation Sacerdotale,* Paris, Lethielleux, p. 141), Canon Lahitton said:

> These doctrines have their parentage in ancient heresies, errors condemned long ago. The attempt is made to base vocations on the inner consciousness of the individual, as formerly revelation was placed there. God, according to the Protestants and the Modernists, speaks to each soul individually, apart from the teaching office of the Church and over the heads of the official dispensers of His divine word. The teaching office of the Church is thus limited to establishing and defining officially what the faithful believe by reason of the diffusion of the interior light that is in them…

Considering only the positive aspect of the question, is it not beyond all doubt that liturgical piety safeguards souls against this danger, and by its collective, hierarchical, external, and official character develops a profound social sense of Catholicism?

Perhaps some will find this asceticism too equalising and democratic, ignoring the distinctions of class which our Lord indicated in the world of grace as in that of nature. There is no reason for this view. We shall show further on how the different states of prayer unfold themselves most wonderfully in the soul that is always united with our holy Church. In fact, the Liturgy recognises many degrees of intensity, many different shades. The light of one and the same sun is reflected with infinite variety, giving life to multi-coloured flowers that possess a charm forever new and to fruit as exquisite as they are various. It is outside these providential inequalities that the liturgical method glories in being popular and universal. Every child of the Church is a saint in the making. *Hence this piety is not reserved exclusively for an ascetic aristocracy,* and is not placed beyond the reach of ordinary Christians. All without distinction, from the Pope to the smallest child learning the catechism, live the same Liturgy in different degrees, participate in the same feasts, move in the same cycle.

Part One: The Restoration of the Sacred Liturgy

One can readily see what a powerful influence this unification of minds and hearts creates in the Church.

4. REALIZATION OF THE SACRAMENTAL RICHES

The Church is the depository and the dispenser of the truth, and the depository and the dispenser of the sacraments as well. It is her duty and responsibility to render these supernatural treasures fruitful, to exploit them for our benefit, to administer them, somewhat as the human hand must turn to profit the bare, natural energies derived from the sun. This is the purpose of the entire sacramental Liturgy, and, to limit ourselves to one point, of the eucharistic Liturgy — that is, of the missal. The latter is the living and authentic commentary of the great Mystery, the language which Christ speaks in His eucharistic silence. Without the Liturgy, the eucharistic reality is, especially for the lowly and the humble, something distant, abstract, impersonal, sometimes monotonous, if not tiresome. By means of it Christ emerges from the immobility and silence of His sacramental state; He acquires all the reality of His life of the Gospels. "Who hears you hears me" (Luke 10:16). I therefore give ear unto the Church speaking to me in the missal; and in the voice of the Bride it is the Bridegroom whom I hear. It is He who prays, who speaks to me in the Gospel; and in all the Masses of the liturgical cycle it is His life that I am living again, and His teachings. Every day the missal presents a new Jesus to my soul, a new mystery, a new word, a new Eucharist. Like His disciples, I find the Master at the well, on the mountain, at the crossroad, on the shore of the lake, at Nazareth, in short, in all the phases of His earthly life. Thus understood, the Mass is an intimate trysting place for us, a living conversation that is ever new, as it was for the disciples of Emmaus: "Was not our heart burning within us, whilst He walked in the way, and opened to us the Scriptures?" (Luke 24:32)

Let us ask ourselves frankly: Has not the missal been to us a closed and sealed book? Why do so many young people, after having spent six or seven years in a house where religion is supreme above everything else, and where every day is begun with the celebration of the holy Sacrifice in the presence of the entire community, consider the Mass with but indifferent fervour, so that they do not assist at it more often than forced to by the law of the Church, and then with the external appearance of a languishing faith?

The Church in her Liturgy initiates us fully into her mysteries: "Let a man so account of us as of the ministers of Christ, and the dispensers of the mysteries of God" (1 Cor. 4:1).

5. METHODS OF INSTRUCTION

Religious education is achieved mainly by the teaching of the catechism, and by the Sunday instruction. We shall see in the chapter on *Liturgy and Preaching* how the Liturgy can be a great help to preachers. Here we shall restrict ourselves to the value of the Liturgy as a method of instruction.

Are the catechism and the Sunday instructions sufficient for all purposes? We think not. Liturgical prayer is our religion in word and act; it is applied dogma, expressed in a language charged with supernatural energies, to which a maximum of intelligent appeal is given by means of all the fine arts. It is the life of Christ reproduced in the liturgical cycle, annually narrated in the Gospels, commented on in the Epistles and homilies, popularised in the lives of the saints, rendered more efficacious by active participation of the faithful in the holy Mysteries — it is Christianity become concrete, condensed, as it were, and prepared for the nourishment of souls.

Christmas teaches us the Incarnation. But this dogma is prayed, chanted; it enters into the song of the Church bells, into the light of a thousand candles. It is dogma felt and lived by the Christian people; and even today, in spite of our surrender of customs and reverence, it is so anchored in our Christian habits that the indifferent themselves and the inimical cannot escape its wholesome influence altogether. This one example alone suffices to show that nothing is so popular and so attractive as the Liturgy, in spite of certain words and gestures to the contrary.

The Liturgy is the catechism of the people; and to help at its restoration is to perform a work that is eminently democratic. Have we not enough evidence for it? To be brief, we shall limit ourselves to the pronouncement of Bossuet at the publication of his *Catéchisme Liturgique*: "You must make them understand," he said to his priests:

> That the Christian year, like the ordinary year, is divided into its seasons, and that the solemnities are distributed over different periods, so that we may in this way be taught what God has deigned to do for our salvation and what is most necessary for us to do in order to attain it.
>
> In fact, if the Christians drew their spirit truly from the feasts, they would lack in nothing that they should know, since they would find in these feasts all the wholesome teachings together with a multitude of good examples.

Further on, in speaking of the catechism, he adds:

> This is a foundation for those whom you instruct, so that for the remainder of their lives they may profitably understand the sermons and assist at the Divine Office with great benefit.

In the catechism of Saint Pius X the didactic importance of the liturgical cycle is emphasised still more:

> The feasts were instituted for the very purpose of rendering a common supreme worship of adoration to God in His temples. The ceremonies, words, melodies, in a word, all the externals, have been so well assembled and adapted to diverse circumstances that the mysteries and the truths of the events celebrated cannot but penetrate into the soul and *there produce the corresponding acts and sentiments*. If the faithful were well instructed, and celebrated the feasts in the spirit intended by the Church when she instituted them, *there would be a notable renewal and increase of faith, piety, and religious instruction: the entire life of the Christian would thereby become better and stronger*...Thus every good Christian, aided by sermons or by some books judiciously chosen, will try to understand the spirit of each feast and make it his own; for that purpose he will learn to know its particular object and end, will meditate on the truth, the virtue, the miracle, or the good deed which it recalls, and *will thus seek to better his life*. He will know God,

our Lord, the Blessed Virgin, and the saints much better, will love them with a more ardent love, and will be led to put their examples and teaching into practice. He will become attached to the holy Liturgy, to the sermon, to the Church, and convert others to his own sentiments. Thus *every feast will be for him a true day of the Lord, a true feast at which his soul partakes of strength and joy, at which he can renew his vigour for the toils and combats of daily life.*

The best way to learn a language is still that of speaking it. Far be it from us to dispute the importance of the theoretical study of the grammar; the latter is evidently indispensable for any intellectual culture. But the question here is of ordinary learning, and from this viewpoint we are making the comparison. Now, it is an elementary pedagogical principle that both adults and children do not learn a language from its grammar; they learn to speak and then speak it. For them this generally suffices. If later they improve their knowledge of the language by a study of the grammar, they must still speak it habitually under pain of forgetting all they learn. This pedagogical method is also that of cultured minds. In general, for learning a language it is necessary to dwell among people that speak it; the best theoretical methods of pedagogy can hardly supply that process.

At the risk of appearing to exaggerate, it is imperative to emphasise the necessity of this principle for the religious education of the people. The catechism, the elementary grammar in our case, is not enough; it is necessary habitually to speak the Christian teachings, and the language for this is the Liturgy. The catechism tells us that the Second Person of the Trinity was made flesh in the womb of the most holy Virgin. This is its formula, and it is necessary; but it does not suffice for the people and the children. However, we have the feast of Christmas, a Christmas eloquent of the past, with its cessation from labour, its nocturnal or morning Office, its three Masses which narrate the whole mystery, its churches lighted up, its joyous chimes and chants, its naïve cribs: a Christmas of long ago, with its echoes ringing at the family hearth and at the family table of poor and rich alike, a Christmas with its accompaniment of Christian joy and life. This is our dogma as the Church speaks of it in the maternal language which we understand so well.

How significant from this point of view is the answer of Godfrey Kurth to the inquiry instituted by *La Croix* into the causes of religious ignorance:

> According to my opinion one of the causes of religious ignorance, if not the greatest, is *ignorance of the Liturgy*...Give the people an understanding, and consequently a love, of the mysteries that are celebrated on the altar; *put into their hands the missal*, which has been replaced by so many common mediocre books of devotion. *This is the true manner of teaching religion*, of attaching those who still visit it to the house of God, of later leading those back who have deserted it *(La Croix, Aug. 5, 1911)*.

Who can not see the immense benefit to be derived from the Liturgy as a means of filling the gaps in the religious instruction of the Christian people, especially today, when the traditional means of instruction are more and more difficult to apply? Today in one country, tomorrow in another, the only religious organism that men have not dared to destroy may be the liturgical gathering. Is not this an additional reason for giving our acts of worship their maximum didactical value?

6. SOCIAL INFLUENCE

Social activities are today one of the most urgently needed forms of the Church's supernatural influence. Without them, the paganism ever hidden in human nature will re-enter the city of God by the devious but sure way which the denial of Christian social principles has opened. The Liturgical Movement glories in having a rôle to play in this gigantic task, a rôle that is a secondary one indeed, but nevertheless unquestionably efficacious. We should like to reproduce here the masterly treatise on this subject given at the 1912 Maredsous "Liturgical Week" (p. 208) by Canon Douterlungne. Only the fundamental ideas, however, can be indicated here:

As a preparation for social restoration, it is necessary to teach the baptised world three great truths: that of the dignity of human nature, that of the brotherhood of man, and that of the spirit of renunciation. In order to spread these truths and endow them with real vitality, not only among a select few, but among Christians in general, the ordinary acts of the Liturgy are a most powerful means.

"The Liturgy," he says truly in concluding the development of his second point:

> Pursues *individualism into its last retreat,* by emphasising so frequently the manner in which the supernatural life is communicated to the faithful soul. The latter receives sanctifying grace as a member of the mystical body of Christ, that is, the Church. This sanctification is not the effect of an exclusive communication of God to the individual man; but, as the sap mounts from the roots to the branches attached to the trunk, so, too, the supernatural life is a sort of common patrimony, which is imparted to the faithful that are in close union, and which passes from Christ to His members. It is not necessary to appeal to the numerous texts of the Proper of the Season, or the Proper of the Saints[5] in order to conclude that the dogma of fraternity breathes from every page of the Liturgy, and that, if individualism and its practical equivalent, egoism, have wrought such great ravages among us, a great reason for this is the abandonment of the Liturgy by the Christians.

In conclusion, the sympathetic director of social action of the Diocese of Tournai addressed the following appeal to his audience:

> Let us spread the *liturgical life;* let us teach the faithful to use the missal; let us introduce the liturgical chant! We shall then have put a leaven into the populace and into the higher social

---

[5] The *Proper* is that part of the Mass and Office of a seasonal feast or of a saint which is peculiar to the feast — over against the *Common* which is the same for various seasons and for various saints (e.g. the Canon of the Mass, which is always the same with the exception of one passage).

spheres, which will sooner or later give rise to good works and completely transform the social sense.

7. APOLOGETIC VALUE

Daily polemics, the hand to hand struggle with the adversary, does not exhaust the mission of the apologist. If it is necessary to conquer truth for souls, it is also necessary *to conquer souls for the truth*. For this peaceful conquest the Liturgy is marvellously adapted; hence from this point of view it can well be defined as *the splendour of revealed truth*.

Of truth, first of all. For its truth is guaranteed by the infallible authority of the Roman Church, the watchful guardian of the canon of Liturgy and of the canon of dogma, having defended the one as well as the other by the anathemas of her Councils. The hierarchical primacy of intellect is therefore preserved in liturgical piety. The latter is piety of the mind before being that of the heart: and to consider it a purely sentimental, aesthetic piety is as unjust as it is injurious to our holy Mother Church.

The Liturgy is also the *splendour* of the truth. From this the positive apologetical value of which we are speaking derives. For the divine prayer of praise which the Church possesses in her Liturgy is of a sublime beauty, embellished by all the reflections of an inspired poetry, both Hebrew and Christian, developed and enriched in the course of centuries, but kept scrupulously pure of all unorthodox alloys.

Shining in its beauty, the truth addresses itself to all the receptive powers of our being, excites religious emotion, intensifies it, raises it to the highest power, and turns it into magnanimous resolutions and energetic acts. Thus we embrace the truth with our whole being, certainly with our understanding, but also with our whole heart and will.

Newman, while still a Protestant, said of the Liturgy that it contained such great excellence and beauty, that if the Roman apologists would hand it to a Protestant as the official book of Roman devotions, this alone would undoubtedly establish a bias in favour of Rome.

While the devotionalism of a mediocre pious literature indisposes or even repels unquiet souls, who have felt a certain longing for God and who have commenced to look back to the old temple, perhaps with distrust, but still with questioning attention, the Liturgy awakens in them a sympathetic curiosity, rehabilitates Catholic piety in their eyes, and at times elicits from them an enthusiastic exclamation like that of Huysmans: "What an immense treasure of poetry and an incomparable domain of art the Church possesses!"

To the artistic and literary appeal, the Liturgy adds the charm, for many souls still more powerful, of a sacred past: "These ancient rites," says Msgr. Duchesne:

> Are doubly sacred, for they come to us from God through Christ and the Church. But they would not possess in our eye such a halo of glory about them had they not also been sanctified by the piety of countless generations. Throughout how many centuries have the faithful prayed in these words! What emotions, what joys, what affections, what tears, have found their expression in these books, these rites, and these prayers! I count myself happy indeed to have laboured in shedding fresh light upon an antiquity thus hallowed *(Christian Worship: Its Origin and Evolution, p. x)*.

If art is indeed a priesthood, then it is above all in the Liturgy that it exercises its ministry.

Chapter V

The Liturgical Movement

"Theoretically," a person may object to the preceding pages, "you are right; your view is unassailable. But is it practicable?" With some such words were the promoters of the Liturgical Movement in Europe confronted in their first attempts, except where they met with downright condemnation. The success of the movement in Europe has given the best answer to the question, which, of course, is a most legitimate one. Theory and practice at times reveal a matter in very different lights.

Let us then be practical. There are thousands of Catholics in this country who assemble every Sunday for the sole purpose of assisting at a liturgical gathering. Presided over by one who is by divine and human delegation the minister of the Liturgy, they assemble in the spacious edifices that were built and consecrated exclusively for the service of God. And they assemble in order to accomplish a work which is, according to Saint Pius X (our theoretical point was conceded above), the primary and indispensable source of Christian life. This is a tangible fact, a material reality, of which we are witnesses every Sunday and every feast day.

Let us make this reality, now insufficiently operative, all that it ought to be: a vital act. It is a practical enterprise if ever there was one! There is no need of a separate calling together of a large number of persevering listeners at the price of efforts sometimes heroic; there are thousands of such groups assembled every Sunday. The programme and the speakers are, for the Christian, incomparable: the drama of Calvary itself, and the ministers of Jesus Christ. The place is provided, so that we are saved the arduous task of building anew. Hence the work can be performed whenever desired; materially nothing will have to be changed.

All is then in readiness; it remains only to intensify the life of this body. Can the *practical* character of such an undertaking be doubted for a moment? It will take time, patience, and perseverance. But everything that is practical requires the collaboration of these three factors — always painful for men of a single day. The hand of time, however, never respects that which men try to accomplish without it. Things of permanent value are achieved only in time.

Saint Pius X undertook this work, which is the most practical of all. He wished to see life breathed into the sluggish body: *"Ossa arida audite verbum Dei:* Ye dry bones hear the word of the Lord" (Ezek. 37:4). Hardly had he been elevated to the Pontifical See, when he aroused the Church by his *Motu proprio* of November 22, 1903, and provoked a powerful movement towards liturgical restoration. This was only one of the many forms, the first in point of time, of an ever more and more marked return to Catholic Tradition.

In order to restore "the true Christian spirit," the Sovereign Pontiff affirmed, it is necessary to lead the people back "to the primary and indispensable source of this spirit; that is, the active participation of the faithful in the most holy mysteries, and in the public and solemn prayer of the Church."

In Belgium and other countries, the Episcopacy answered to the instructions of the Head of the Church, and, thanks to its initiative, Catholic activity has developed far in this direction. Under the impulse of His Eminence Cardinal Mercier, the Catholic Congress at Malines, held in September 1909, used the occasion for uniting those of good will, for determining upon a summary programme in the form of resolutions, for arousing the attention of men of action, in fine, for creating a Liturgical Movement.

The movement developed rapidly and multiplied its methods of action. Reviews and publications of all kinds, liturgical and Gregorian "weeks," congresses and "days," committees and circles of liturgical study, a general secretariat, were instituted — in fact, all the various enterprises of which the Benedictine abbeys of Belgium became centres, and which gave the movement such a profound and efficacious vitality.

The spirit of this movement is well brought out by an episcopal letter of His Eminence Cardinal Mercier, whose encouragement was so urgent and wholehearted:

Part One: The Restoration of the Sacred Liturgy

Then the liturgical traditions will be renewed. Souls will again live the 'liturgical life.' Gradually the faithful will again learn that Jesus Christ is 'the Way, the Truth, and the Life.' The cycles of the year will recall the succession of the 'mysteries' of the birth, the apostolate, the redemption of our divine Saviour.

And every time the faithful yield to the attraction of Him who said, 'And I, if I be lifted up from the earth, will draw all things to myself,' and go to assist at the mystical renewal of the sacrifice of their redemption, they will approach nearer to our Lord by their love and their faith. Then, when they communicate at the hand of the celebrant, they will understand better that the price of their admission to the eucharistic Banquet is the redeeming sacrifice, the kiss of peace which the eternal Father extends to His restored and repentant children.

Now silently, now by chanted prayer, they will respond together to the invitations which the priest extends to them from the altar; and this pious interchange between the pastor and his flock, between the flock and their pastor, will consolidate the family bond in our parishes, and will strengthen the Catholic sentiment of the Communion of Saints in souls.

The work which the monks of Mont-César have undertaken under your wise direction is beautiful and highly meritorious, Right Reverend Abbot. God will bless it. It must succeed. For my part, I wish it a broad diffusion among the parishes, in the religious communities, in the colleges of my diocese. I am firmly confident that the intelligent title that was chosen for this publication, *Vie Liturgique*, is prophetic of a happy reality.

The programme of the movement was formulated piecemeal, on different occasions and in various articles and publications. We shall take the liberty to put together the complete plan of action here, and in a few lines to mention both the end it pursued and the desired reforms.

Liturgy the Life of the Church

The central idea to be realised by the Liturgical Movement is the following: "To have the Christian people all live the same spiritual life, to have them all nourished by the official worship of holy Mother Church."

The means to be employed towards this end are of two kinds. The first have reference to the acts of the worship itself; the others to the liturgical activity exercised outside these acts.

Acts of Worship. In this field, the members of the Liturgical Movement desire to contribute with all their strength to the attainment of the following aims:

1. The active participation of the Christian people in the holy Sacrifice of the Mass by means of understanding and following the liturgical rites and texts.
2. Emphasis of the importance of High Mass and of the Sunday parish services, and assistance at the restoration of the collective liturgical singing in the official gatherings of the faithful.
3. Seconding of all efforts to preserve or to re-establish the Vespers and the Compline of the Sunday, and to give to these services a place second only to that of the holy Sacrifice of the Mass.
4. Acquaintance, and active association, with the rites of the sacraments received or assisted at, and the spread of this knowledge among others.
5. Fostering a great respect for, and confidence in, the blessings of our Mother Church.
6. Restoration of the Liturgy of the Dead to a place of honour, observance of the custom of Vigils, and Lauds, giving greater solemnity to the funeral services, and getting the faithful to assist thereat, thus efficaciously combating the de-christianising of the rite of the dead.

Liturgical Activity outside of acts of worship. In this field there are four ways in which the members can assist at the furtherance of the Liturgical Movement:

A. *Piety.* 1. Restoration to a place of honour among Christians of the traditional liturgical seasons: Advent, Christmas Time, Lent, Easter Time, octaves of feasts, feasts of the Blessed Virgin, the Apostles, and the great missionary saints of our religion.
2. The basing of our daily private devotions, meditation, reading, etc., on the daily instructions of the Liturgy, the Psalms, the other

Part One: The Restoration of the Sacred Liturgy

liturgical books, and the fundamental dogmas of Catholic worship.
3. Reanimation and sublimation of the devotions dear to the people by nourishing them at the source of the Liturgy.
B. *Study.* 1. Promotion of the scientific study of the Catholic Liturgy.
2. Popularisation of the scientific knowledge in special reviews and publications.
3. Promotion of the study and, above all, the practice of liturgical prayers in educational institutions.
4. Aiming to give regular liturgical education to circles, associations, etc., and to employ all the customary methods of popularisation to this end.
C. *Arts.* 1. Promoting the application of all the instructions of Saint Pius X in his *Motu proprio* on Church music.
2. Aiming to have the artists that are called to exercise a sacred art, architecture, painting, sculpture, etc., receive an education that will give them an understanding of the spirit and the rules of the Church's Liturgy.
3. Making known to artists and writers the fruitful inspiration to art that the Church offers in her Liturgy.
D. *Propaganda.* 1. Using all means to spread popular liturgical publications that show the import of the principal part of the Liturgy: Sunday Mass, Vespers, Sacraments, Liturgy of the Dead, etc.
2. Reawakening the old liturgical traditions in the home, that link domestic joys with the calendar of the Church, and using for this end especially the musical works composed for such purposes.

    To all Catholics we address a burning appeal in favour of the activities that aim to realise as far as possible the programme of liturgical restoration we have here outlined.

PART TWO

THE SECONDARY MISSIONS OF THE SACRED LITURGY

This second part, which can be omitted by the reader pressed for time, connects the liturgical apostolate, of which we have spoken, with other essential phases of the life of the Church and of souls.

The cursory considerations that follow do not pretend to be complete. Mere sketches, they will nevertheless suffice to dissipate more than one misapprehension, and to inspire men with a more sympathetic attitude towards the Liturgical Movement.

Chapter VI

The Liturgy and Asceticism

1. Notion of Catholic Asceticism.
2. The Liturgy in Relation to This Asceticism.

1. NOTION OF CATHOLIC ASCETICISM

Asceticism, in general, is the totality of the practices *(askesis* — exercise, training) that aim to subjugate the flesh and to ensure the dominion of the spirit. More simply, it is the predominance of the higher life in us through the sacrifice of the lower. The man who is in league with his spirit against his own flesh is an ascetic.

This definition is applicable to all forms of asceticism. The recluses of the temple of Serapis devoted themselves to all sorts of austerities, and with unpitying fanaticism strove to attain the death of the senses *(apatheia* — insensibility) in order to give dominion to the spirit.

The *end* of asceticism is, therefore, to realise in oneself both a death and a life — with more or less thoroughness and abundance according to the fervour and enthusiasm of the person practising it. The *means* are a series of exercises and acts that tend to realise this death to self and this new life. In a restricted sense, the term *asceticism* is often applied to this series of practices; sometimes merely to those relating to the body.

Christ, God-man, is super-eminently the pure, the supreme Ascetic beyond compare. The mystery of death was realised unto the sacrifice of the cross; the mystery of life, unto the exaltation of His glorious humanity. And the practices which brought about this triumph of life over death embraced the most generous and the most fervent of human efforts. By its grandeur of purpose, of means, and of accomplishment, the life of our divine Saviour is so transcendent, that one can, nay must, call it the uniquely ascetic life: our Lord is *the* Ascetic *par excellence.*

There is a still higher truth in this. Christ is the ascetic *par excellence* not only by the intrinsic transcendence of which we have spoken, but still more so because His death, His life, the act which realised them, His asceticism in short, is in principle and right also ours, that of all His members: "Buried together with him," "planted together in the likeness of his death," "crucified with him," etc. (Rom. 6:4-6). His asceticism is essentially a collective work, one of substitution; He died *in* our *stead*. There is, then, in the New Dispensation an authentic asceticism for us, which associates us completely with the passion, the death, and the resurrection of Jesus Christ, and which we can achieve by the authentic means He has instituted for this perfect assimilation. In this sense, which alone is the true one, every Christian is an ascetic, the more so the more truly he associates himself with the death and the life of Jesus Christ.

Now, the primary institution by means of which Christ wishes to unite us with the mystery of death and of life, is the holy Eucharist taken in all its plenitude as Sacrifice and Sacrament. *There* is the true source of Catholic asceticism. It is precisely by means of His eucharistic state that the divine Ascetic wishes to transform us into Himself. All our sacrifices and our mortifications will then be offered at the altar of the one Sacrifice by which our death is rendered acceptable. On the other hand, the correlative mystery of life, which constitutes the positive aspect of this asceticism, is not realised in all its fullness of conservation and growth except in the sacrament which consummates the sacrifice. It is the life of God that penetrates us, that transforms us, and that leads us towards the full life of eternity: "He that eateth my flesh...hath everlasting life and I will raise him up in the last day" (John 6:55). We sacrifice an inferior for a superior life, for the life divine, and all through Christ, with Christ, and in Christ, to the glory of the Father. *Such is the soul of Catholic asceticism.*

The *end* of Catholic asceticism being thus fixed, let us glance at the *ascetic means* to be used in the New Dispensation — the exercises proportionate to this end. The first is *prayer*. The Christian ascetic will be, above all, a man of prayer. Through supernatural help alone can he remain faithful to this law of death unto himself and of life unto God, without which there can be no asceticism for him. In a state of natural asceticism, such as paganism conceived, there was no question of this primary element. For the Catholic, on the other hand, "to learn to pray well is to learn to live well" despite Pelagius. Besides, prayer naturally requires effort, and is even in so far ascetic.

The second indispensable means for the *ascetic disciples of Christ* is the fruitful *contemplation of the mysteries,* the teachings, and the examples of our Lord's life, in which they must learn to put off the old man and to live the new. The model of the divine Ascetic must be placed before their eyes. It must radiate in all its living splendour, in order to excite love and enthusiasm and energetic resolutions in them. And for arousing their courage and facilitating imitation, they must contemplate the lives of the saints, their precursors and models in the asceticism of Christ.

Thus prepared, they will bravely enter upon the *material and moral practices* by means of which man submits the flesh to the spirit, and the spirit to God. If they desire to practice the ordinary asceticism, they will observe the commandments of God and of the Church, and the practice of the virtues which these commandments require: prayers, penances, fasts, alms, continence. What efforts, even these, for realising in themselves the mystery of death, and of life in God! Undoubtedly every Christian is an ascetic. And if his soul is filled with special heroism and enthusiasm, and if the grace of God abounds in him, he will embrace still greater sacrifices, mortifications more thorough. Then the mystery of death and of life will be fulfilled by the vows of religion; he will be a complete ascetic, a perfect Christian.

But in order that these practices enter completely into the *Catholic ascetic dispensation,* they must take on the aspect of sacrifice; they must be centred about the altar, accomplished under the impulse of the virtue of religion, commanded by the latter; they must in some way become acts of worship. The perfect ascetic gives this character to them by elevating them to the level of religious vows.

Such is, in brief, the complete notion of Catholic asceticism. Let us summarise it in a few words:
1. *End:* To die and live with Jesus Christ in the Eucharistic Sacrifice.

2. *Means:* a. Supernatural aid through prayer; b. Fruitful contemplation of the life of Jesus Christ; c. Material and moral practices calculated to subdue the flesh and the spirit; d. The vows of religion for the most perfect alignment of our asceticism with the eucharistic Sacrifice.

2. THE LITURGY IN RELATION TO THIS ASCETICISM

The rôle of the Liturgy in all this is easily seen. We shall consider it in relation to the end and the means we have indicated.

1. *End. Sacrifice* is the primary act of worship, and the eucharistic Sacrifice is the *centre of the worship of the Church*. The Liturgy gives its full value to the element of sacrifice and intimately associates all the faithful with this central hearth; the altar is the axis around which the entire liturgical prayer revolves. And since for the Christian ascetic the eucharistic altar must be the tryst whither he comes daily to receive the basic lesson of the oblation of self by virtue of the example of the gift of his Master, is it not true to say that the Liturgy, in giving to the Eucharist, Sacrifice and Sacrament, all its powerful efficacy over our souls, is the *universal and official school* of true asceticism?

Hence any diminution of liturgical piety marks a weakening of the idea of the eucharistic *Sacrifice,* and therefore of the very foundation of the ascetic life. In our opinion there is no greater evil than this in modern piety. The element of sacrifice inherent in the Eucharist has been lost; or men consider it a ritual act which hardly concerns them, or in which they themselves have nothing to sacrifice. Few enough, to our knowledge, truly live the eucharistic Sacrifice, feel that they are embraced in its action, or there offer with Christ all the sacrifices that fidelity to His law will demand in the course of the day which is commencing. Few enough advert to the fact that in default of the ancient offering of wheat, of wine, of wax, as symbols of the oblation of self, the Church wishes that the action of the offertory suggest to us to give ourselves. For God reclaims us, God awaits us, us above all, His ascetics, who wish to die entirely with Him.

Catholic asceticism and the Liturgy therefore have the same focal centre, the same foundation, the same soul; namely,

Part Two: The Secondary Missions of the Sacred Liturgy

the eucharistic Sacrifice. Whatever loss the Liturgy suffers among Christian people is also a loss of the notion of sacrifice, and consequently of Christian renunciation.

In reviving an understanding and a love of the eucharistic Sacrifice, Saint Pius X recalled the people to the source of asceticism. The ideas of the faithful are not sufficiently enlightened upon this point, and more than one pious soul would perhaps be scandalised to hear that the *chief* aim of our Lord in instituting the Eucharist was not that of being a permanent Host in our tabernacles, but that of *realising every day and in every member of Christ the mystery of the death and the life of the Head by means of the eucharistic Sacrifice and Sacrament.*

The faithful do not doubt that their priests are performing a eucharistic work of the first order — more essentially eucharistic than many other excellent but secondary functions that are cultivated too exclusively — whenever these priests try to create a more intimate contact between the celebrant and those assisting, to lead those assembled to enter into the reality of the Sacrifice, to give new life to the torpid body that is present at the parish High Mass. Sometimes the eucharistic worship is made to consist of a multiplication of benedictions, of expositions, of nocturnal adoration. Men forget too readily that the first duty of the apostle of the Eucharist is to emphasise the active participation of all in the solemn Sacrifice of the Day of the Lord, as the most important universal act of religion, and to procure this participation not through means devised by personal zeal, but through those indicated by Saint Pius X in his plan for the restoration of the Liturgy.

To give *more* solemnity and splendour to Benediction than to holy Mass, to *accustom* the Christian people to low Masses that are as little solemn, and as short as possible — a true liturgy of the catacombs and the persecutions — and, on the other hand, to inculcate the greater importance of the benediction services by means of an intense publicity, of musical selections of every kind, choice sermons, electric illuminations, ornamentation mountain-high, in fact by means of all the modern resources of attraction; to turn the main altar into a rich support for the tabernacle, often also a mere pedestal for some saint; to transform the altar, sanctified by the solemn lustration and anointing of the pontiff, the inviolable reliquary where the bones of martyrs rest, the symbolical stone,[1] which we kiss with love and which we salute and incense with reverence, the mystical Calvary where our Saviour renews all His wonders — to transform this most sacred object of the sanctuary into a terraced stand covered with candles and flowers, or even to disguise it for a month at a time: all these abuses and so many others, contrary to the prescriptions, the principles, the spirit of the Liturgy, in time affect the mentality of the faithful, relegate to a place of minor importance the primary aspect of immolation and union with God, lose sight of the essential act of our worship, reduce the Eucharist merely to a real Presence or a sacred Repast, stripped of all further more sacred aspects that the eucharistic Mystery realises.

If the Liturgy has been called a method of asceticism, this means, among other things, that it presents the death and the life of our Lord, renewed and communicated to us in the real sacrifice of the Mass as the foundation of the daily practice of renunciation and mortification: *hostia pro hostia* — victim for victim.

It is this great and fruitful principle of an asceticism specifically Christian that the Church, in the person of the ordaining pontiff, proposes to all her ministers on the day of their priestly ordination: *Agnoscite quod agitis, imitamini quod tractatis: quatenus dominicae mortis mysterium celebrantes, mortificare membra vestra a vitiis et concupiscentiis omnibus procuretis.*[2] An admirable programme of ascetic life, derived from the eucharistic Sacrifice, the centre of the Liturgy: Sacrifice Jesus Christ every day, that His sacrifice may become yours; die with Him to sin. Every day at the altar renew your desire to be ascetics; *imitamini quod tractatis:* imitate what you perform.

2. *Means.* Being intimately associated with the *end* of asceticism, *the four means* enumerated above likewise receive an increased efficacy from the Liturgy. We shall give only a few indications thereof:

---

[1] *Altare Filius Dei est (Pontificale Romanum,* ordination of subdeacon): The Altar is the Son of God.
[2] "Bear in mind what you do. Imitate what you perform, so that in celebrating the mystery of the death of our Lord, you take heed to mortify your members of all vices and concupiscences" (Ceremony of Ordination).

Part Two: The Secondary Missions of the Sacred Liturgy

a. The first care of the ascetic must be to attain a most intimate contact with all supernatural realities, above all with the action of the Holy Ghost. But as we have mentioned often enough, the prayer of the Church realises this contact with a degree of perfection and abundance that is unequalled elsewhere; it submits us directly to the action of the Spirit who gives life. Thence the ascetic, who has professionally vowed himself unto things perfect, will apply this same professional care to attaining perfection in the domain of piety; he will have a predilection for perfect piety, for liturgical piety, which gives to this first means of ascetic Christian life its maximum of efficacy.

b. The second means for the ascetic is the contemplation of the mysteries of Christ, with a view to imitating them in life. Each mystery, each page of the Gospel, lives again in the liturgical cycle. It is read to us at the altar, for it must transform itself into sacrifices in our souls. The Church draws from each mystery a virtue to be practised, a victory to be gained, a sacrifice to be united to the great Sacrifice. In fine, after unfolding the entire mystery with a sumptuousness truly royal and causing it to be contemplated in all its aspects, the Liturgy deduces practical applications, precise reforms to be effected in our life, which are expressed in the collects, the secrets, the homilies;[3] *quod recordatione percurrimus...opere teneamus.*[4] The Liturgy makes us contemplate with fervour and enthusiasm, in order to correct us and inspire us with energy and perseverance. And if the soul is sincere and loyal, it can not fail to respond to the practical conclusions so forcefully present in the prayers and the mysteries it chants: *vide ut quod ore cantas corde credas et quod corde credis operibus comprobes:* See that what you sing with your lips you believe with your hearts, and what you believe with your hearts you manifest in the conduct of your life (Roman Pontifical).

We are here face to face with one of the most persistent prejudices against liturgical piety; namely, that it supposedly

---

[3] *Collect* is the name given to the official prayer of the Mass recited after the Gloria or Kyrie; the *Secret* is a similar prayer recited before the Preface. The *Homilies* are the sermons of the Church Fathers on the Gospels, constituting lessons of the Divine Office.

[4] What we contemplate in mind, may we put into practice.

promotes a sentimental and sterile contemplation without practical effects, without the fruits of interior reform, without ascetic value — like Rachel, beautiful but sterile. More, however, than any other method is the piety of the Church a lever, a crucial insight. For in these "ineffable sighs of the Holy Spirit in us," are prepared conversions, resolutions, better lives, efforts towards sanctity. The imitation of the mysteries of Christ is natural and easy for the ascetic who associates himself sincerely with the prayer of the Church. Upon this title rests the claim of the Liturgy to asceticism.

c. As to the ascetic practices themselves, the efforts and mortification of all sorts undergone for the attainment of virtue — fasts, vigils, penances, alms, continence, vows of chastity, of poverty, of obedience — in short the whole array to the number of seventy-two which Saint Benedict in chapter four of his Rule calls *instrumenta artis spiritualis* (instruments of the spiritual art) and which are sung three times a year at the Benedictine Office of Prime — none of these ascetic practices are formally acts of worship. Hence they do not depend upon liturgical activity.

We may nevertheless remark, without pausing longer over the point, that the Liturgy in the institution of Lent, of the Ember Days, the Vigils, the consecration of virgins, the monastic professions, and numerous other rites and texts, creates an environment that is very propitious for these practices of asceticism, and gives them a positive and supernatural import, pivoting them around the centre of all Catholic asceticism: assimilation with the sacrifice of Jesus Christ. Those who have doubts on this point will do well to read the excellent report of Msgr. Harscouet on this subject in the *Semaine Liturgique* of Louvain, 1913.[5]

d. Finally, the complete ascetic life is intimately related to liturgical piety by means of the *Vows of Religion*. Thanks to these vows, the life of the chosen ascetic becomes a continuous homage to the Most Holy Trinity, an anticipated dedication, which is a prelude to that of eternity. All renunciations become so many means that increase the dignity of the worship of God; they

---

[5] Cf. *Des Semaines Liturgiques: Louvain du 10 au 14 Août 1913*, Abbaye du Mont-César, Louvain 1914.

enhance the acts of the virtue of religion; they are so many additional sacrifices. In this respect, also, the two activities join hand, for the Liturgy realises the same attitude in the soul: by its means the Church, Spouse of Christ, takes up all her children in her arms, offers them day and night to the glory of the Father, the Son, and the Holy Ghost, consecrates them to the worship of the thrice holy God. Hence, also, does the profession made by the monk unfold its action in harmony with the different phases of the eucharistic Sacrifice: *the ascetic, like the priest, is bound to the altar.* Excellent words on this subject have been written in the remarkable volume of Dom Morin.[6]

Before entering upon this relation, it will be well to mention that liturgical piety creates a *state of soul that is singularly favourable to a most whole-souled asceticism.* The irreconcilable enemy of spiritual dryness, of isolation, and of laxity, which weigh down and fatigue the wings, it gives to truth and virtue all the captivating embellishments of the arts. By its living forms it satisfies all the capacities of understanding and of love in our being and gives warmth to souls by a contact so close that there is "but one heart and one soul." In true motherly fashion it causes us to live in joy, in abundance and in peace; it dilates the heart and teaches us to speed with running feet on the path of asceticism. *"In via mandatorum tuorum cucurri, cum dilatasti cor meum:* I have run in the way of thy commandments, when thou didst enlarge my heart" (Ps. 118).

Dom Morin has also written some excellent pages on the rôle that joy plays in the ascetic life *(ibid.* chap. xi) ; and in them he comments on the passage of the Acts: *"Sumebant cibum cum exultatione:* they took their meat with gladness" (Acts 2:46). These pages must be meditated if the immense ascetic value of liturgical prayer, from this secondary viewpoint alone, is to be appreciated. There is the time of Easter, for instance. Amidst such resources of asceticism, what a flood of joy it pours into the hearts of those who have been resuscitated! It is over fifteen centuries ago that our brethren at Hippo experienced this same enthusiasm, so

---

[6] *The Ideal of the Monastic Life Found in the Apostolic Age,* Benzinger, New York 1913, chapter iv.

fruitful of action: "Therefore, well-beloved," Saint Augustine addressed them:

> Let us praise the Lord, repeat Alleluia! Let us in all these days symbolise the day that will be without end, hasten our march towards this eternal habitation. Happy those, who dwell in Thy house, O Lord; they shall praise Thee for all centuries! Yes, we shall enter into this house, which is heaven. There we shall praise the Lord, not for fifty days (Easter Time), but, as it was written, 'during all centuries of centuries;' we shall see, we shall love, we shall praise…all will be eternal, all will be without end. Let us praise, yes, praise! But praise not only with our voices, also by our works; may our lips praise, may our life praise, and may it be animated by the love that is not extinguished!…Oh! what happiness there will be, what tranquillity, in chanting the Alleluia! Here we chant it; but it is in the midst of our cares; there it will be in peace…Here we chant on the way, there in our home. Now, then, let us chant, brethren, not to conjure up repose, but to alleviate our work. Sing…sing and march on…" (P.L. t. 38, col. 1185).

Hilarem datorem diliget Deus, the Lord loveth a cheerful giver. To sing while giving oneself to the Father through the sacrifice of Jesus; and to sing better in order to give better — such is at once the charm and the reward of an asceticism inspired by the Liturgy.

It is therefore unquestionable that the Liturgy, properly understood and lived, is a superior school; that since the beginnings of Christianity spiritual athletes, ready for the glorious battles of the ascetic life, have issued from it. More fortunate than the old pagan disciples of Serapis, completely penetrated by a wise ascetic strategy, they learn by a living instruction which issues from the lips and the heart of a mother — and what a mother! — that the act of dying and living, to which they dedicate themselves, draws its efficacy and its virtue from the eucharistic Sacrifice fully entered into; that the spirit of prayer and the fruitful contemplation of Jesus are elements of Catholic asceticism, as indispensable to the latter as are the personal efforts of their own supernaturalised selves; finally, that

Part Two: The Secondary Missions of the Sacred Liturgy

these efforts must rise to the height of religious motives, that is, to the virtue of religion, in order to attain the perfection of the sacrifice of Jesus Christ.

Chapter VII

The Liturgy and Prayer

1. General Ideas on Prayer. 2. Relation to the Liturgy.

1. GENERAL IDEAS

1. By the superior activities of his soul every man must unite himself to the Sovereign Good as intimately and frequently as the individual and social contingencies that regulate his momentary existence here below permit.

What is to be said, then, of the soul that has professed to live for God alone in this life? Such a soul will have no activity more habitual and more spontaneous than that of daily more completely appropriating unto herself, by acts of understanding and will, the sole True, and the sole Good, her sole Heritage.

2. The activities of the intellect are multiple. It abstracts, thinks, reflects, meditates, contemplates, sees. The will in turn is moved, desires, loves, longs for, decides, acts, and causes all things to act. In the New Dispensation these supernaturalised faculties, without having lost anything of their spontaneity, are by the help of grace employed in the search for their God, *"per vicos et plateas quaeram quem diligit anima mea:* In the streets and the broad ways I will seek him whom my soul loveth" (Cant. 3:2). In ordinary language one word suffices to designate all these operations and these infinitely varied strivings of the superior faculties of our souls for God, and that is: *Prayer*.

3. In its variations prayer is therefore unlimited. Each of the above acts can lead the soul to union with God. There the soul can then stop, there rest at its pleasure; its end has been attained. But this is only one of the special kinds of prayer. The classification can go on *ad infinitum*.

Classification is, however, a delicate task, capable of disconcerting the most experienced psychologist. And the reason is that consciousness, *in its palpitating reality,* is not a chess-board with compartments rigidly separated from one another. It is rather like a flowing stream, uniting in its turbulent current the many smaller streams that rush into it from the elevations and are there swallowed up without giving either their name or their course to the main stream.

To speak without figure, it is difficult to classify the different kinds of prayer. In fervent souls, sincere and unaffected, the different acts succeed one another without regard to our classifications or gradations: the sight of a flower throws Saint Francis into ecstasy.

This reservation understood, we shall briefly enumerate some of the varieties of prayer.

4. The truth that engages the spontaneous activity of our intellect in reference to union with God can come from without; and it is then transmitted through the senses to the intellect whose nourishment it becomes. For this it is necessary to read, to hear, and above all to pray for the grace of understanding. He who act thus, undoubtedly practices prayer. (See no. 2.)

5. The internal activity of the intellect under the inspiration of truth, and that of the will under the influence of good, may be translated into external action in song and vocal prayer. For this man may either improvise the expression of his sentiments, or appropriate, and make his own, formulas that are used for this purpose. There is no doubt that this action is one of prayer. Intellect and will are really united to God; and the soul is not content to remain quiet in its possession, but chants forth its joy, shouts out its love, in the holy formulas it borrows for this purpose. This is prayer. If there is any divergence of opinion in the matter, it has reference not to the objective reality of the fact, but only to the word that is used to designate it.

6. Before going further, we may remark that in the two above acts of prayer the external plays an essential rôle, either as point of departure (no. 4) or as terminal point (no. 5). After them commences the purely interior prayer, in which external things play only a secondary part. This type is called *mental prayer*, also simple *prayer*.

Mental prayer is then the activity of a soul that is assisted by grace, and is ever desirous of uniting more intimately with God — *a purely interior and private activity, a sort of silent and untrammelled recollection in God.* This ascetic exercise is not and cannot be a formal liturgical act. It is interior, private, spontaneous, and free, while every liturgical act must be externalised, public, hierarchical, and official.

7. Man can ever better assimilate the truths he possesses by faith. His soul conceals treasures of life which he must exploit by an interior activity that constitutes a mental prayer. To this end the intellect, with the assistance of grace, reflects, analyses, synthesises, and draws conclusions, which the will lovingly undertakes to realise. The truth is transformed into resolutions and acts. By reason of its deductive procedure, this mental prayer is habitually given the name of *meditation.* Various methods can be employed to organise this interior activity of the soul and to intensify its results. It is not our task to attempt a comparative study of these different methods. May we not hold in practice that the best is the one that most profits the soul using it? The confessor would seem to be the surest counsellor in this matter.

Objection has been made to this mode of prayer on the score of its dryness, and its ready forgetfulness of supernatural co-operation. But we must keep in mind the important remark made above (no. 3). Deductive methods do not necessarily exclude the other activities of intellect and will.

8. The intellect in possession of the Sovereign Truth can pause before this Truth, long its object of meditation, in order to regard It with an enduring and unchanging gaze, and to enjoy It. The will can find its pleasure and repose in the Good possessed. This method of mental prayer is *contemplation* properly so called. Its variations are graded indefinitely according to the intensity of divine grace and the fidelity of our Christian life. Are not mystical states simply higher degrees on this same ladder of perfection? This question, with so many others, concerns the authorities on asceticism; it is beyond our present scope.

Saint Francis de Sales *(Treatise on the Love of God,* vi, 3) has well characterised the state of contemplation in its relations to the preceding method: "Contemplation is nothing but the loving, simple, and permanent attention of the soul centred on things divine. Prayer is called meditation until it has produced the honey of devotion; after that, it becomes contemplation."

Part Two: The Secondary Missions of the Sacred Liturgy

9. Before examining the relation of the Liturgy to prayer, it will be opportune to say a word about the *time* to be fixed for the latter, since that question has also been raised in discussions on liturgical piety.

The man who wishes to live fully for God will seek to raise his intellect and will as often as possible to Him who is the object of all his desires. He will be a man of prayer, under whatever form it may be. Union with God will be habitual for him; it will be his breath, his life. And his spirit of prayer, that is, union with God, will in his eyes add new colour to all things.

Vowed to God and desirous of this complete union of the soul with its Creator, he will, if possible, choose a state of life favourable to this union: separation from the world, abandonment of all worldly cares, complete mastery over all his senses, solitude, silence, a life of mortification — in short, the life of the ancient ascetics, the monastic life organised by the Church and following definite rules, all of which agree on the essential principles of which we have spoken.[1] In a life that has preserved this ancient organisation, there can be no question of fixing a definite time for *prayer:* this would be equivalent to depriving the hours not appointed of such a prerogative. Prayer must be the breath of the monk: his active life, his studies of theology, of the Psalter, the Sacred Books, his readings of the Fathers — all this is done for union with God, which result he obtains spontaneously, without constraint, without artifice, without tension of spirit. *His whole life is wisely and discreetly organised for the attainment of this ideal.*

For those, on the other hand, who by vocation and apostolic mission mingle with the world, monks, religious, secular priests, or lay people, it is absolutely necessary to set a fixed time for prayer. This is especially true of present-day life, in which participation in the acts of the Liturgy is so reduced and the activities of life are growing more and more absorbing, so that without such definite periods of time the faithful and fervent

---

[1] These words are meant primarily for those who feel the special call to the life of complete renunciation. For the many who must remain in the world, and who are equally beloved of Christ, the above words are *proportionately true.* All are called to attain the spirit of their divine Master. — Tr.

performance of prayer is endangered. I say *prayer,* wishing to indicate thereby that every one must, according to the impulses of grace, choose the method which, with the advice of his confessor, seems most suitable.

From all that has been said, the falsity of the prejudice is evident, which claims that the different activities of the soul embraced under the term *prayer* are of relatively recent origin, and that they were not in use among the ancient monks, since their monastic rules do not mention them nor fix a special time for them. Prayer is as old as asceticism itself, of which it is an indispensable element. Only, *men of old were less occupied in defining and analysing it than living it.* The monastic rules fixed neither the length nor the time of prayer, no more than the doctor prescribes a daily walk in the fresh air for the hardy peasant, who fills his lungs with the bracing air of the mountain and the forest; or than he prescribes a yearly stay at the seashore for the fisherman and the sailor.

For all those who live in the vitiated atmosphere of the world, it is necessary to observe scrupulously the habit of daily renewing their spirit in prayer, and of annually restoring their energies by means of a spiritual retreat.

2. RELATIONS OF THE LITURGY TO PRAYER

We shall here indicate three principal relations, which well merit the attention of the reader.

1. *The acts of the Liturgy superior to prayer.* All the acts of the Liturgy, in so far as they are acts of the visible priesthood of Jesus Christ, and independently of other treasures they may contain, are of a different order and on a different level from the activities of the soul which we have grouped under the general term *prayer.*

Indeed, any comparison is here unjustified and useless. The acts of the Liturgy, understood in the broad sense that we have sufficiently indicated above, derive all their power of sanctification and of intercession from the fact that they are the authentic priestly acts of the visible hierarchy. Through them Jesus Christ fulfils the work of His priestly mission; the Holy Spirit acts on souls; the Church puts into play the full efficacy of

Part Two: The Secondary Missions of the Sacred Liturgy

her priestly powers: in them we reach the source of supernatural life. The more we participate, with body and soul, the more we draw life from this source.

2. *The acts of the Liturgy constitute prayer.* The same liturgical acts, which we have viewed above in their hierarchical and sacerdotal aspects, can also be of great importance from another point of view, however the latter may be secondary in relation to the former.

The performance of the liturgical act taken by itself, that of the priest at the altar, of the monk at his Office, also constitutes prayer. This becomes evident when we apply the general ideas on prayer mentioned above.

The act of the priest at the altar, and of the monk at his Office, is not mental prayer (purely mental) for the reasons mentioned above (under no. 6). It is, above all, an act of the Church herself, and on this score possesses a far greater efficacy. But does it not come under any one of the forms of prayer? Without a doubt it belongs to the types mentioned in paragraphs 4 and 5. The liturgical act is an act of prayer. The faculties of the soul are engaged upon truths and upon formulas that are imbued with the Catholic spirit; these truths awaken faith in us, and incite us to repentance and to love.

Everything is done for intensifying their action in us. We know, on the one hand, that they are laden with graces. On the other hand, in externalising our interior prayer, we are placed under the control of the Church and in contact with the assembly of the faithful. The liturgical acts, therefore, furnish an excellent means of union with God in prayer for those who perform them with attention and fervour.

The words of Saint Pius X in his bull *Divino afflatu*[2] are very significant. The restorer of traditional prayer shows there how the Psalms contain an element of prayer of the highest order. "Among other things," he says, "there is in the Psalms a surprising power *to stimulate souls to a love of all the virtues.* Indeed, who is there that does not feel himself moved by the numerous passages of the Psalms, where time and again the

---

[2] Cf. Braga & Bugnini, *Documenta*, pp. 111-119; ET: Seasolz, *The New Liturgy*, pp. 22-35.

immense Majesty of God is sung in the most sublime terms, His Omnipotence and His Justice, His Goodness, His ineffable Mercy, and His other infinite attributes? Whose heart does not echo with like sentiments during these songs of thanksgiving for *the* favours received from God, of humble and confident prayer for new benefits, of soulful cries of repentance over sins? *Who is not filled with admiration* at hearing the Psalmist now recount the great gifts received from the divine Munificence either by the people of Israel or by the entire human race, and now unfold the truths of divine Wisdom? And who, finally, does not feel his heart vibrate with love before the image of Christ so faithfully portrayed, of Christ, whose voice Saint Augustine (In Ps. 42, n. 1) heard in all the Psalms, now chanting praises, now singing, now telling of hoped-for joys, and of sorrows endured at present?"

Do not these different acts of the soul under the influence of the Psalms, recited or chanted, constitute an excellent prayer?

The Sovereign Pontiff appeals to the testimony of the Fathers of the Church, Saint Athanasius, Saint Augustine, Saint Basil, etc., who affirm the ascetic value of the Psalms:

> It is Saint Athanasius who says so pointedly: "It seems to me that the *Psalms ought to be as a mirror to him who chants them:* in the Psalms *he must think of himself and of the sentiments of his own heart;* and he must chant them in this disposition." Saint Augustine likewise writes in his *Confessions:* "How often I have wept under the strong emotion of Thy hymns and of Thy canticles, the melodious voice of Thy Church! These sounds ring in my ear, and through them *the truth unfolds itself in my heart;* they *give birth there to sentiments of ardent piety,* the tears flow from my eyes, and these tears are a joy unto me" (Lib. IX, cap. vi).

Would that we could often have such fervent prayers!

Among the advantages to be derived from the liturgical acts performed in this spirit of prayer, we can mention the following: (a) an efficacious remedy against routine and indifference; (b) a ready source of rich and fruitful sentiments which are sought in vain elsewhere; (c) the assurance of abundant

Part Two: The Secondary Missions of the Sacred Liturgy

graces for intellect and will by virtue of the power of the Church's prayer. Further development is not necessary.

One important remark, however, is in place while we are viewing the acts of our worship from the standpoint of prayer. We shall borrow it from a work of rich ascetic value by Dom Festugière *(Essai de synthese,* p. 72):

> Those who dispute the aptitude of the Liturgy for giving the soul vivifying religious experiences are out of touch with the conditions necessary for the success of such experiences. In fact, they generally divide the daily exercises of piety into two classes: *Those that are lived* (meditation, prayer) and those that are performed or gone through, as we may say, for 'quieting conscience' (the breviary). There are ecclesiastics, highly respectable, who would not take away a single moment from their regular time of meditation — and they do well — in order thereby to 'gain' two or three minutes on the time needed for the recitation of their canonical hours. But it is furthermore necessary to recognise that there is an infallible way of annulling the value of the Office as a course of religious experience; and that is to make the recitation of this Office an exercise of volubility. How differently the Saints recited the Office — the blessed Curé of Ars, for example!
>
> *A distinction of a semi-juridical, semi-ascetic nature* will be of good service here in clarifying our question. Moral theology has given us the norms which express the *minimum* of conditions that the cleric must fulfil in the recitation of the Office, which will ensure a performance of this duty that is satisfactory in conscience. But let us persuade ourselves — and how important this point is in regard to religious experience! — that the Office recited well from the canonical standpoint (without fault) may be liturgically recited badly (without spiritual benefit). The *obligation has been satisfied (satis-facere:* to do enough), but there has been *no gain.* The law has been fulfilled; but the devotion has been empty.
>
> There are very pious men who do not draw any spiritual nourishment from this Liturgy, to which the precept of the Church constrains them, and they exclusively seek elsewhere

for the food of their souls. The attitude may even become part of a veritable system of spirituality, adopted with deliberation and in all good faith. The divorce between 'social' prayer and 'individual' prayer is pronounced without appeal. The spiritual life is cut in two by a rigid separation. Evidently such a *dualism* places the religious experience of the persons succumbing to it in conditions that are quite different from those which a state of *homogeneous spirituality* would have produced."

3. *The Liturgy favours mental prayer.* The acts of the Liturgy are not and can not be purely mental prayer, as we have said above in no. 6 of this chapter. But the Church by her liturgical prayer also teaches her children how to pray in the interior recesses of their hearts.

Let us indicate the truth of this briefly for the two principal types of mental prayer, to which the other types can ultimately be reduced: that which proceeds by way of reflection, of methodical deduction, and which is called *meditation;* and that which commences where the above ends, which fixes the intellect upon the truth rendered habitual to the soul by many previous acts of reflection, and which simply regards its object with a silent continuous sentiment of love for the truth contemplated — called therefrom *contemplation.*

But does not liturgical prayer hinder these different degrees of prayer rather than favour them? For meditation it is necessary to reason deductively and to conclude with a practical resolution. What, then, some may ask, can the Liturgy, which inclines towards digressions and sentimentalism, do in an atmosphere so thoughtful and positive? Its activity is that of the cricket and not of the ant! On the other hand, since in liturgical prayer the soul, ever exuberant, appeals to all creatures to go to God, and lives in the constant society of men and angels — will not the ascetic therein lose his facility for the attitude of contemplation in which the soul, stripped of all else and resting in itself alone, fixes its vision immovably on God in enduring bliss?

Quite the contrary! After the Liturgy has held its disciples in a vivifying and intimate contact with the priesthood of Jesus

Part Two: The Secondary Missions of the Sacred Liturgy

Christ, after it has taught them to perform all the liturgical acts, Mass, Breviary, administration of the sacraments, etc., in a spirit of prayer, after securing these two primary and essential results of its method, it has a further salutary influence to exercise on this interior activity of the soul that in the silence of mental prayer strives for a more intimate union with its God. Indeed, we believe that the soul formed in liturgical prayer will possess a facility of communion with Heaven, a pliancy and fervour, which will make its hours of prayer more spontaneous and more sweet.

A. *Development in regard to meditation*. Meditation is classed among the exercises of mental prayer, being a work of interior reflection upon, and of deduction from, the truths possessed by faith. Still, in meditating, a book is often used, which serves as an incentive or as a means of training one's thoughts or guiding them. Hence nothing in this method of prayer is opposed to the use of liturgical books as matter of prayer. It is this point alone that concerns us here.

The special methods that can be followed in this practice of reflection may vary indefinitely. Once it is acknowledged that there is sufficient matter in liturgical prayer, the latter can accommodate itself to any method. There is only one preference to be expressed in accordance with its spirit; namely, that the daily meditation should occupy itself preferably: (1) with attempting to understand the daily lesson taught by the Liturgy, drawing the practical resolution suggested thereby; (2) with the attempt, made in a spirit of faith and of love, to fathom the sacred books that are used in the Liturgy, and especially the Psalter, of whose value for prayer we spoke above; (3) with the attempt to understand the great dogmas that are the foundations of liturgical prayer.

But this preference should be understood as not being narrow or exclusive. Who would think of rejecting the *Imitation of Christ* or so many other ascetic works?

Our choice of the matter for meditation offers immense advantages which we shall here point out in brief.

a. *Guarantee of orthodoxy and of pure devotion*. The soul quenches its thirst at the fountain of life. When souls that meditate do not possess the resources and the security derived from serious theological studies, they incur the danger of entering upon a wide stretch of land alone and without compass. The flat sentimentalism that is found in certain modern manuals of devotion will help us understand the advantage of the above guarantee.

b. *Riches and abundance of texts.* The liturgical passages are taken from Holy Scripture and the Fathers, and proposed for our devotion by our holy Mother Church. They are replete with the mentality of the ages of faith, full of the grace and charm of the literary and artistic treasure they love to employ. What titles, these, to our practical veneration and to our zealous confidence!

c. *Methodical distribution.* Apart from the liturgical cycle, the only factor that regulates the sequence of daily meditation is the subjective plan adopted by the person meditating, or used by the author of the book that has been chosen. Some caprice or other, printer's rules, an accidental circumstance, causes a change in the manual and often produces an entirely new arrangement of its contents; and it is the spirit that thereby invariably suffers loss. Why thus play about from path to path, when our Mother Church has in her cycle solicitously indicated to us an annual itinerary of spiritual renovation?

d. *Homogeneity of spirituality.* The faithful, desirous of perfection, must above all participate in the liturgical acts as often as possible and as actively as possible; this is well understood. For reasonable creatures, this activity implies first of all the co-operation of intellect and will. In order, then, to safeguard the fulfilment of the principle just enunciated, our souls are obliged to imbue themselves with the thought, the sentiments, the examples, which explain to us the mysteries celebrated and the lessons read in these liturgical acts. If the meditations fill our souls with thoughts, sentiments, temporary inspirations, quite different from those which the Liturgy evokes, the only result is one of confusion and embarrassment that is very disadvantageous to our piety. Liturgical piety is homogeneous; our acts of worship and our meditations mutually assist one another: there is peace in our souls.

e. *The importance of the liturgical acts safeguarded.* In order to regain the peace disturbed by the dualism mentioned above, the soul might unconsciously diminish the attention given to the thoughts and the sentiments of the Church. But the liturgical life would instantly begin to suffer and to languish. In place of a fervent participation, eager, with tense soul and ardent heart as at Emmaus, there would be an assistance less and less active and zealous. We know the rest. The liturgical piety, on the other hand, is far from incurring such a danger; by its method of meditation it secures that most active participation which is the "primary and indispensable source of the true Christian spirit."

f. *Guarantee against routine and formalism.* This evil, it must be confessed, is frequent in the acts of worship. Between the official and the artificial there is more than one tie. And the evil is a sad one; the assistance of the faithful at the Sunday Mass suffers greatly therefrom, to mention only one instance. There is only one remedy: learn to understand and to love. The Church knows her children well when she so lavishly gathers into her liturgical books treasures that are ever new and never exhausted. Every Mass of the missal is a vein of gold running close to the surface; all that is necessary is to extract it and to stamp it into coins. Liturgical piety does this, and therefore constitutes an efficacious remedy against the evils we have mentioned.

g. *Unity intensified.* We shall not prolong this enumeration, which is, in reality, only indicated here. Before concluding, however, let us emphasise the greatest of all the advantages, that of the increasing union with our holy Church, and thence the consciousness, ever more distinct and efficacious, of the Communion of Saints. We are at present in the Octave of the Ascension,[3] a period that was for all times consecrated to prayer and recollection by the last word of our Lord to His Apostles a moment before His Ascension. The Church preserves this sacred character in her Liturgy of the time; she prays the same prayer with all her children, asks the same Gift, sings the same triumphs, makes us feel this perfect unity of the mystical body, which gives such joy and courage to the soul. Unity with the whole past — such has been the prayer for centuries; unity in the present — all the children of the Church are called to live this same life; unity in the future — the traditional spirit of the Church guarantees this, all Christians that shall succeed us to the end of time will pray thus. But liturgical piety also tends to intensify this

---

[3] This chapter first appeared in a Belgian liturgical periodical. — Tr.

incomparable good more and more by entering more intimately into this union through daily meditation. At the same time, what comfort for the soul, depressed and saddened by isolation, to be able to comprehend so well, by means of meditating and living the Liturgy, this all-powerful, supernatural current in which it is borne along!

B. *Development in regard to contemplation.* In this domain more than in any other it is necessary to look at everything in a broad spirit of faith and from the supernatural point of view. But if the Liturgy of the Church is, according to the beautiful expression of Saint Pius X in the bull *Divino afflatu*, the voice of the Church and the daughter of heaven; if, as we sing in the beautiful hymn of the Dedication of the Church, the Liturgy makes us the emulators of the angels: *illi canentes jungimur almae Sionis aemuli* — joining heaven's ranks in emulating praise; if, in a word, it realises all that we have tried to say here, how can anyone hold that those who wish to practice and live it fully are not entirely prepared for a life of more unitive prayer, distant foretaste of the joys of heaven, which will unfold itself in the company of the angels for all eternity?

The soul that places herself under the influence of the Eternal Priest by means of the Liturgy of every day and every hour, becomes the voice of the Church, and thence of the Holy Ghost. From her lips and her heart issue the psalmody and the holy readings with which the Holy Spirit at one time inspired the seers; she abandons herself in a spirit of faith and love to the Mother of Saints, in whom the great stream of supernatural life circulates. Can not the soul that lives thus draw from this habitual intercourse the ardent desire and the divine strength to contemplate Him with whom she entertains herself intimately at all hours of the day and of the night?

To ask the question is to answer it; and one can not be sufficiently on one's guard against the contrary illusions. Rather than develop the theoretical reasons for this efficacy here, we shall cite a practical application from the report of Dom Ryelandt given at the 1912 Maredsous Liturgical Week *(Cours et Conférences,* p. 183). It will be a happy conclusion to what we have said in this chapter:

Part Two: The Secondary Missions of the Sacred Liturgy

What the holy Liturgy teaches us in an excellent manner is prayer. It teaches prayer, not by reasoning with us, by demonstration, but by a procedure that is peculiarly its own: it suggests the attitudes of the sincere soul. In placing the formulas of her own prayer on our lips, the Church tends to put the holy dispositions of mind, which these formulas express, directly into our souls: interior acts of humility, of contrition, affections and acts of love, of praise, of acknowledgement, of union of our will with God, etc. *Quod os dicit, cor sapit:* What the mouth speaks, the heart feels.

Is it not that to which all the methodical considerations given in books tend? Do they not attempt to provoke movement of the soul, affections, resolutions, by means of general considerations and of three special points?

The Liturgy reaches the same end, but by a shorter path, by suggesting the dispositions of soul of which we have spoken.[4]

Let us suppose someone reciting the Office and speaking to himself, from the bottom of his heart, the words that his lips murmur: *A custodia matutina usque ad noctem speret Israel in Domino:* From the morning watch even until night let Israel hope in the Lord (Ps. 219:6).

Now, supposing that after the end of the Office or the Psalm, the soul continues in this holy sentiment, and that in order to repel distractions and to retain the spark of love and of confidence contained in it, the person repeats this verse, or some other prayer of similar trend, softly from time to time; such a one will have an excellent prayer.

This same method of prayer can be renewed for other verses, whether they express the deliverance into the hands of God: *Jacta super Dominum curam tuam et ipse te enutriet.* —

---

[4] Undoubtedly the spiritual life must be based on solid convictions, but these convictions need not *necessarily* be acquired during the half-hour of meditation. The reflective study of theology, personal reflection on the events of life, on one's readings, on the Liturgy, can engender these dispositions outside the time of meditation.

Obumbrasti super caput meum in die belli: Cast thy care upon the Lord and He shall sustain thee (Ps. 54:23) — Thou hast overshadowed my head in the day of battle (Ps. 139:8); or excite to fidelity, or speak of repentance, of pure love: *Quid mihi est in coelo et a te quid volui super terram?* For what have I in heaven? And besides thee what do I desire upon earth? (Ps. 72:25). Read the penitential Psalms and you will experience in the depth of your soul a spirit of compunction, which will cause you to say with your heart rather than with your lips: *Domine, ne in furore tuo arguas me;* or *Miserere mei secundum magnam misericordiam tuam:* Rebuke me not, O Lord, in thy indignation (Ps. 31, 1); Have mercy on me according to thy great mercy (Ps. 50, 1). These interior attitudes, inspired by the Psalms and the Liturgy, constitute true prayer. If they become in reality cries of the heart that suffers, or trustful acts of submission, acts of love, or resolutions always to do the will of God, they will be the more useful for the spiritual life. Let us then open our souls with a recollected and respectful spirit, in order to receive these holy inspirations. And having received them, let us guard them as a precious grace which must fructify our life in order to bring it into an ever truer union with God.

Chapter VIII

The Liturgy and Preaching

1. General Ideas on Preaching.
2. The Liturgy in Relation to Preaching.

1. GENERAL IDEAS

1. The teaching of Christian doctrine to the faithful by a consecrated minister in virtue of the hierarchical power, which he possesses over them either in his own right or by delegation, is called preaching. It is essentially the exercise of a spiritual power. The preacher has the right to instruct the faithful; the latter have the duty to learn from his word.

2. Considered in itself, preaching is not a liturgical act. We said above that the Liturgy is an incomparable method of instruction; and in this wider sense we can say that the whole Liturgy preaches. We are treating here, however, of that exercise of hierarchical authority by which a spiritual minister explains to those who depend upon him spiritually — preaching properly so-called. And in this stricter sense it is not necessarily an act of worship.

3. I have said 'necessarily,' for it can happen that in the very exercise of a liturgical function the Church imposes upon her priests the charge of addressing the faithful and exhorting them to receive with devotion the sacrament about to be conferred, etc. Everyone knows that our liturgical books contain many examples of this strictly liturgical preaching, whether the text is absolutely fixed, or whether room is left for a spontaneous exhortation on the part of the priest. The obligatory homily which follows the Gospel at the Sunday Mass belongs to this same category, but in a wider sense.

2. THE LITURGY IN RELATION TO PREACHING

From the foregoing it is evident that a close relation exists between these two priestly powers. I shall indicate it briefly here, leaving entirely out of consideration the doctrinal and pedagogical value of the Liturgy, which is treated elsewhere.

1. *The Liturgy is the occasion for preaching.* The sermon requires an audience: a place, an assembly that is ready, a background; and these are furnished by the Liturgy. The same commandment that gathers the faithful around the altar every Sunday for the eucharistic Liturgy, groups them by that very fact around the chair of instruction.

The desertion of the Sunday Mass necessarily also engenders religious ignorance. The pastoral influence exercised by sacred preaching is in direct proportion to the diligence with which the faithful participate in the liturgical services. The moment that the assistance at these services is minimised or disappears — to the detriment of the parochial church — the pastor, however eloquent he may be, loses contact with his flock. The desertion of his church and his services automatically creates a void about his chair.

In passing from the altar to the pulpit of truth, the priest does not interrupt the liturgical action. He there appears endowed with all the prestige of the sacrificial priest, vested in the liturgical garments. It is the preparatory Mass that is taking place; the instruction is embodied in the fore-Mass, the Mass of the Catechumens; and the profession of faith, the Credo, which is chanted in unison, is an echo of the teaching of the pastor.

The faithful approach God by acts of adoration and praise, and God comes to them by the grace of truth — and the mediator of this divine exchange is ever the priest, whether he is at the altar with hands elevated towards heaven, or in the pulpit with the divine word on his lips.

Was it not in the liturgical gatherings of the Jewish Sabbath that our Lord and His Apostles found their most favourable opportunities for preaching the Gospel? Hence even from this viewpoint preaching is guided by the Liturgy. But this is evidently only a very secondary relation.

Part Two: The Secondary Missions of the Sacred Liturgy

2. *The Liturgy matter for sermons.* Our liturgical books contain a vast number of rites and ceremonies that symbolise religious truths, a cycle of annual solemnities that revive among us the entire work of the redemption, a wonderfully rich storehouse of phrases and readings, all breathing faith and love. Illuminated by their light, warmed by their ardour, the priest feels the energies of his spiritual fatherhood awaken; his children must partake of his life. His heart is filled to overflowing; his lips speak of its fullness. Such is the origin of the homily, which existed in practice long before it was found in any code of regulations. It was the universal custom of the churches that gave rise to the ancient discipline regarding the homily still in force today.

The primitive Christian literature is very suggestive in this regard, so that the liturgical canon of some of the churches could be reconstructed from a study of the homilies of their pontiffs. Among the Fathers of the Church there are especially two popes whose teachings display the strongest liturgical character, both of them great persons in the history of the Church: Saint Leo and Saint Gregory. Every year we see them penetrate deeper into the mysteries which the successive stages of the liturgical cycle propose for our meditation.

"While I know well, dearly beloved brethren," says Saint Leo in his third sermon of Epiphany:

> That your saintly minds are not ignorant of the object of today's feast, and that the customary reading of the Gospel has explained it to you, nevertheless I shall attempt to say to you that which our Lord suggests to me, so that you be not deprived of that which we owe to you in virtue of our charge.

This is but one example among a thousand. The entire patrology from Saint Clement to Saint Bernard confirms our position: the little that we read in our breviaries suffices to establish it.

The Council of Trent has insisted on this point of discipline, and Saint Pius X reminded the clergy of it in his encyclical *Acerbo nimis* of April 15, 1905. The Fathers of the Council expressed themselves as follows:

Even if the Mass should contain great instruction for the faithful, still it does not seem expedient to the Fathers that it be celebrated in the popular tongue. Hence retaining the rite everywhere approved by all the churches of old, and by the holy Roman Church, the mother and teacher of all the churches, *lest the sheep of Christ hunger and the little ones ask for bread and there be none to break it for them,* the holy synod commands all pastors and those having the care of souls to explain frequently during the celebration of Mass in person or by others, from among those things that are read in Mass, and among other things something also of the mystery of this most holy Sacrifice, especially on Sundays and feast days.

Echoing these words of the Council, the catechism *Ad parochos* reminds pastors that the ceremonies used by the Church, especially in the administration of the sacraments, were instituted for a triple purpose: to secure for the holy mysteries the religious respect that is owing them, to instruct the faithful, to excite in them sentiments of faith and love. It concludes by saying that the priests must have at heart the duty of getting the faithful to understand the ceremonies of the worship.

The same catechism arranges a table for the use of preachers, in which to each Gospel of the Sunday are added these lessons of the catechism that can serve as inspirations for the liturgical homily. The Liturgy thus serves as a chain with which the religious instructions are inter-linked.

The same interrelation is expressed in numerous rubrics of the *Ceremonial of Bishops.* Among other passages we read: "There should be a sermon on the current Gospel regularly within the Mass" (Bk. I, ch. xxii, no. 2).

Those who still doubt the efficacy of liturgical preaching may with great benefit read the conferences of the Reverend M. Brassart at the 1912 Maredsous Liturgical Week, (pp. 228-275), in which the unforgettable speaker, with his fine sense for contingencies and possibilities and his charming humour, indicated the resources which the Liturgy offers to sacred orators. We cannot but quote some suggestive lines here:

Part Two: The Secondary Missions of the Sacred Liturgy

But the liturgical riches are not contained merely in the Psalms. *Everything in the Liturgy is divine praise, dogma, or moral truth* under the form of prayer, which consequently should impress itself on our souls in outstanding characters. Nowhere else will you find the essence of our religion presented to the people with such skill, force, and simplicity. The examples are abundant. Let us choose the virtue of humility. By what means are theologians initiated into the science of humility? By means of definition, division into different classes, the methods of acquiring it, the manner of practising it. Many volumes have been written on this virtue. How many pages in St Thomas or in Rodriguez, or in no matter what book of meditations! If the people must know these ideas in order to understand humility, and to practice it — and this is necessary since the proud are excluded from the kingdom of heaven — how are they to acquire them? Fortunately we have the Liturgy. Without occupying itself with scientific methods, it goes straight to its task, and that in a forceful manner, direct and comprehensible. It instructs the people in a concrete fashion and one entirely within the grasp of their minds. As examples, it is sufficient to read and comment on (a) the parable of the Pharisee and the Publican; (b) the advice of Christ to those who are invited to a banquet; (c) the washing of the feet at the Last Supper: *The Son of man is not come to be ministered unto, but to minister*; (d) the dispute of the Apostles over precedence, as well as the request of the mother of the sons of Zebedee: *Say that these my two sons may sit, the one on Thy right hand, and the other on Thy left, in Thy kingdom*; (e) the words of Christ when He took a child, embraced it, and placed it in the midst of His disciples: *Unless you become as this little one, you will not enter into the kingdom of heaven*. You may aspire to be the first, but have a care, convert at once; if not, you shall not enter into the kingdom of heaven! Do you not find that this poor human pride, so strongly denounced by the Gospel, truly comes to nought? You will nowhere else find a theological treatise on humility so beautiful, so sublime, and so well adapted to the understanding of the people.

Nor do the other virtues fare less well. The Liturgy lived! This is the Christian life in its entirety, with its difficulties and its victories; it is unshakeable confidence and joyous enthusiasm even amidst the miseries of this world here below. Does it not constantly hold up to Christians the magnificent recompenses that Christ has reserved for His servants? Christians of ordinary intelligence, who are absorbed in the numberless cares and occupations imposed upon them by their positions in life, would become most fervent souls if every Sunday they should abstain from servile work, assist at services by following the liturgical prayers, and profit by the simple and obvious explanations of their pastors. In the Liturgy everything is said so well, all is presented to the people in so telling a manner, there is a mine so rich and so easily exploited, that we are tempted to say to the authors of books intended for the instruction of the people: Cease this effort, it is in vain; the Liturgy has done the work much better than you shall ever be able to do it.

Chapter IX

The Liturgy and the Science of Theology

1. *General Ideas on the Science of Theology.*
2. *Relation of this Science to the Liturgy.*

1. GENERAL IDEAS

1. The human intellect essays to study the revealed doctrine transmitted by the teaching office of the Church. Thanks to all the work of reasoning, of deduction and co-ordination, of analysis and synthesis, regulated by the laws of logic, it succeeds in organising a science, in constructing a system. This is the science of theology, which is characterised differently according to the special objects it studies: dogma, moral, etc.

2. The theological treatises, therefore, give a scientific and logical exposition of dogma and moral *(logical* in the philosophical sense of the word). They do not formally aim at the practical organisation that is proper to an art: *scientia, non ars:* a science, not an art.

3. *The liturgical books,* on the contrary, are *not scientific treatises* of revealed truth. From this viewpoint they are in a class with the Gospels, the Epistles of Saint Paul, with all books that aim at a practical and living realisation of their content: *ars, non scientia.*

4. When, therefore, we say that the liturgical books are truly handbooks of dogma and of moral, we are imitating the ordinary language that calls the Gospel a code of morals, or an Epistle of Saint Paul a treatise on grace, etc. To conclude from this innocent manner of expression that the Liturgical Movement wishes to have the liturgical books adopted as manuals for teaching, is to interpret it with a scrupulous rigor that would suppress all orthodox license of style.

5. The liturgical books must be, and are more and more getting to be, an object of science; that is, of liturgical science, which has its own procedure, methods, auxiliary sciences, and

which differs in object, method, and procedure from the theological sciences of dogma and moral.

6. The promoters of the Liturgical Movement in no way desire to diminish the capital importance of the present teaching of theology. If they had a wish to express in this matter, which belongs exclusively to the hierarchy, it would be on the contrary, that dogma teaching be developed more than ever, according to the spirit so insistently pointed out by the saintly Pius X in his encyclical *Pascendi:* "Evidently more importance must be attached to positive theology than in the past, but without the least detriment to Scholastic theology. And those must be reprimanded as doing the work of Modernism, who extol positive theology to such an extent that they seem to decry scholastic theology at the same time."

7. While moving in distinct domains, however, Liturgy and dogma have points in common which we shall now briefly indicate.

2. RELATION OF LITURGY TO DOGMA

1. *The Liturgy is tributary to dogma.* In his *Motu proprio* of Nov. 22, 1903, Saint Pius X starts from the principle that the Liturgy aims at "the glory of God, the sanctification and edification of the faithful." The Liturgy is therefore a factor in our religious life; it is a supernatural activity. Now, the primary element of our supernatural life is faith; and our entire activity in this field rests on the revealed truths to which we adhere by faith. It is evident from this that the Liturgy must be built up on our Credo as on its indispensable foundation; it is our faith confessed, felt, prayed, chanted, brought into contact with the faith of our brethren, of the entire Church. Dogma is to the Liturgy what thought is to the orator, what the ideal is to the artist.

Furthermore, the first condition of a system of worship is that it be *true*. It must, above all, take into account the nature of God and that of man, the relations which it has pleased God to establish between Himself and His creatures, our situation in relation to God. It is dogma that reveals this nature to us, that defines these relations and determines our religious attitude. Religious worship, and *a fortiori* the worship of our holy Church,

Part Two: The Secondary Missions of the Sacred Liturgy

which is the Liturgy, must be completely tributary to dogma under pain of being false and useless. Hence it is a liturgical work of the first order to seek the nature and laws of this dependence. How could the Liturgy attain its end, which Saint Pius X tells us is to glorify God and sanctify men, if it were not above all theological? Glorification is *notitia cum laude:* knowledge with praise; sanctification has faith as its root — and both of these presuppose a doctrinal basis as indispensable.

It is evident that in the liturgical texts dogma is not presented under the form of theses and canons. For this purpose the Church exercises her *munus magisterii,* her teaching office, in its various forms. But the Liturgy assimilates dogma, adapts the latter to its nature, and expresses it in formulas, rites, and symbols.

This continual dependence is attested by history. The evolution of the living Liturgy went through the same vicissitudes and stages as did the dogmatic development. As soon as a dogma became more precise in doctrinal teaching, the liturgical formula took on the same character. Arianism had used the formula of prayer addressed to the Father, *per Christum Dominum nostrum:* through Christ our Lord, as a pretext for denying the divinity of Christ. Immediately a second part of the conclusion came into liturgical use...*qui tecum vivit et regnat,* who liveth and reigneth with Thee. The Pelagian errors led to a continuous appeal to divine assistance; and the use of the versicle, *Deus in adjutorium:* O Lord, come unto my assistance, was multiplied. But we cannot stop here.

In contemplating the powerful structure of our Catholic cathedrals, do we ever think of all the laws of architectural technique, of all the scientific principles regarding the equilibrium and the resistance of various materials, of all the geometric theorems and algebraic formulas, that are applied? Undoubtedly not. They are there nevertheless, regulating the entire construction, governing all the details of the shape and the place of every stone, thus assuring the stability and the preservation of the edifice. The eye does not discern them; hardly does the mind of the ordinary person suspect them; they are as the invisible soul of the body of stone. Thus it is with the Liturgy. Dogma is everywhere; and it is not a mere part. It inspires and regulates the least gestures and least formulas, both with discretion and with minute care. The Liturgy is theology, not scientifically expounded, but applied to the art of glorifying God and sanctifying souls.

2. *Dogma tributary to Liturgy*. The liturgy in turn renders two important services to dogma in the life of our holy Church. *It gives testimony of dogma,* and its testimony is without appeal; it popularises dogma by introducing it into the mind, the heart, the soul, of the faithful with consummate pedagogical skill. It has been called the theology of the people. This latter aspect we have developed above; we shall here say a word about the former.

The Liturgy gives testimony of dogma. The liturgical books constitute a theological source that is of the greatest value. In the famous controversy of the nineteenth century in France on the matter of the return to the Roman Liturgy, Dom Guéranger developed this dogmatic value of the Liturgy in all its fullness. His study takes up the entire fourth volume of the *Institutions Liturgiques*.[1] All the misconceptions and objections are there expounded at length in three public letters by Msgr. Fayet, Bishop of Orleans, and the author of the *Institutions* undertakes a methodical refutation of them. We cannot think of summarising the powerful study here; but we urgently advise those interested in this theological question to ponder it thoroughly. The Liturgy there stands out from the narrow and depreciating conception of mere ceremonialism, and appears as the principal instrument of the Tradition of the Church. The author cites a great number of writers in confirmation of his view. We shall mention a few of them.

In his polemic against quietism, the enemy of every *request* made to God, Bossuet emphasises its opposition to the teaching of the Church. One of his arguments runs as follows:

> The principal instrument of the Tradition of the Church is contained in her prayers. Whether we examine the action of the Liturgy and the Sacrifice, or pass to the hymns, the collects, the secrets, and the post-communions, it is

---

[1] Vol. IV, 2 edition, Paris, 1885, p. 243-583.

remarkable that not one can be found which is not accompanied by express requests.[2]

Dom Guéranger cites many extracts from the illustrious polemicist, and concludes by saying: "I shall not multiply further these quotations from Bossuet, of which I could give twenty pages." The learned Renaudot, in his magnificent collection entitled *Liturgies Orientales*[3] gives a still more complete exposition of the *dogmatic value* of the Liturgy:

> If there is one point that possesses superior authority in the solution of questions concerning faith and discipline, it is surely the testimony of all the churches, registered from ancient times on, and perpetuated and renewed in the succession of the ages. In this category there is the ancient tradition, which is of great weight, as also the writings of the Fathers whenever they are in agreement on the principal matters of faith and of discipline. Finally, there are also the decrees of the Councils and the other ecclesiastical writings. *But among all these documents, those that represent the voice and the testimony of the whole Church have supreme dignity, for they were known and approved in all places, and contain not only the testimony of bishops but also of the people. Such are the liturgies, of which we have just treated, and whose importance comes not so much from the names to which they are attributed as from the common use of them by the churches, which employed them at the altar for so many centuries.*

The entire exposition is nothing more than a commentary on the celebrated text attributed to Pope Celestine (d. 432), in his letter to the bishops of Gaul:[4]

> Let us attend to the meaning of the priestly prayers, which were received in the entire world as the tradition of the Apostles, and which are uniformly in use in the entire Catholic Church. From the manner in which we must pray, let

---

[2] *Etats d'oraison*. Bk. VI, ed. Migne, 1856, t. iv, col. 115-116.
[3] Vol. I, Francfort, 1847. 2 ed. p. XLIX.
[4] Ep. 21, chap. ii, Migne. P. L., t. 50, col. 535.

us learn that which we must believe: *Legem credendi statuat lex supplicandi.*

The Tradition handed down by the organ of public prayer is thus unanimous, universal, hierarchical, and official — so many qualities that give to a theological source all its value. Tell us how Augustine of Hippo, Ambrose of Milan, Isidore of Seville, Gregory of Nyssa, Chrysostom of Constantinople prayed, and we shall tell you the *Credo* of their respective Churches. Thus the progress of liturgical studies will have its counterpart in the field of theology. To give only one example, the theologian who ignores the recent liturgical works on the sacraments exposes himself to grave misconceptions in a study of the subject.

To resume our comparison, if the immense Gothic cathedrals conceal principles and laws of architectural technique, which give the edifices all their consistency but are not seen or suspected by the uninitiated, these in turn become for the practised eye an unquestionable document, which permits the reconstruction of the entire science and of all the formulas that guided the genius of the architect in the complicated construction of this skeleton of granite.

Conclusion

The author recalls a tour in which the members of the party visited the sumptuous church of Saint Mark's of Venice. The visit was hurried and distracted, after the general fashion so well known to fatigued tourists who have gone over the customary itinerary of Italy in a similar manner. In this sudden vision Saint Mark's appeared to him as a grandiose heap, somewhat fantastic, with its endless colonnades, its ancient vestibule, brilliant cupolas, polychrome marbles, rich mosaics, its entire Byzantine splendour. Of this hasty and superficial inspection nothing but a confused impression remained, a vague memory, without unity and coherence. Nor could the *cicerone* with his avowed admiration and banal explanations arouse any enthusiasm. Still the first visit created a desire to return to this marvel so sparingly viewed and to contemplate it at leisure.

Later on, the author had the opportunity to admire this incomparable work for long hours at a time. Even from a distance a multitude of prophets, apostles, and saints, chiselled in marble and porphyry, call the Christian to adoration and prayer. When he enters the edifice, his ravished eye discovers a new procession of them, more fervent, more sumptuous still, whose majestic theme is developed on the pillars and the vaults of the porticoes, on the golden background of the mosaics, on the bas-reliefs of the portals of bronze, on the long balustrades and stalls, down to the very pavement, where they walk on foot, bearing with them in their march the entire history of the creation and of humanity, and extending their universal homage to the very centre of all these splendours, the main altar, more rich, more scintillating than all the rest, with its baldachino of porphyry, its heavy strips of gold, its *pala d'oro*, all studded with gems and precious stones. And what riches and priceless works, not suspected by the profane visitor, are hidden in its treasury, its sacristies and museums!

Although all these beauties unfolded themselves to the ravished eyes, one idea dominated the author's thoughts, which served to increase the general impression: for him Saint Pius X, pope scarcely a few months, still lived in his beloved basilica. Here the echo of his voice resounded; his great soul still animated it. The great pontiff had known all the splendours and had loved them; and better than anyone else he understood their language. This remembrance made them doubly dear and sacred to the author.

In completing these too hasty pages, in which the Liturgy appears like a bird in flight, the reader will also regret the hurried march and the curt information of his *cicerone,* and will search his mind in vain for a general plan, only to feel the impression of a thing hinted and guessed at. May he at least derive from his reading the conviction that the treasures of supernatural life and of Christian renovation are hidden therein; may he return often, very often, to the same topic, but then under the guidance of masters!

The piety of the Church, of which Saint Mark's is but the symbol, will then appear to him in its powerful unity of doctrine and life. In the Liturgy, too, everything leads us to the central hearth of the eucharistic Mysteries. Readings, chants, prayers, psalmody, hymns, antiphons, sacramentals, and blessings — each of these leads the soul to Jesus Christ, gives it life, and immolates it with Him to the glory of the Most Holy Trinity.

In it all the good things come to us through the Roman pontiff; they would be without value in our eyes, did they not receive their supreme consecration from the authority of the Vicar of Jesus Christ, the unique Pontiff.

Like the wonderful basilica, the Liturgy has riches and splendours of infinite variety in reserve for all souls, and for all circumstance of life. Yes! Would that the preachers explained it, the educators taught it, the theologians consulted it, men of action propagated it; that mothers spelled it out and children mouthed it; that ascetics there learned true sacrifice; Christians, fraternity and obedience; men, true equality; and societies, harmony! May it be the contemplation of the mystic, the peace of the monk, the meditation of the priest, the inspiration of the artist, the magnet that draws the prodigal! May all Christians, hierarchically united to their pastor, to their bishop, to the common father of the faithful and of their pastors, live it fully, come to draw the true Christian spirit at this "primary and

Conclusion

indispensable source", and by means of living the Liturgy, realise the prayer of the first Mass of the eternal High Priest: *Ut sint unum,* that they be one — supreme wish and supreme hope!

That is the Liturgical Movement; *all* of *that; nothing but that!*

The Benedictine Abbey
of Saint Michael at Farnborough
was founded from the French
Abbey of Solesmes in 1895. The monks live
a traditional life of prayer, work and study
in accordance with the ancient
Rule of Saint Benedict.
At the heart of their life is the praise of God
expressed through the solemn
celebration of the Sacred Liturgy,
and supported through their work,
of which this publication is an example.